RESTORATION

Village

RESTORATION
Village

Philip Wilkinson

Photography by
Peter Williams

ENGLISH HERITAGE

First published 2006 by English Heritage, Kemble Drive, Swindon SN2 2GZ
www.english-heritage.org.uk

10 9 8 7 6 5 4 3 2 1

A CIP catalogue record for this book is available from the British Library.
ISBN-10: 1 873592 97 3
ISBN-13: 978 1873592 97 7
Product code 51213

The BBC logo and the 'Restoration' logo are trademarks of the
British Broadcasting Corporation and are used under licence.

©BBC 1996

©BBC 2003

This book is published to accompany the television series Restoration Village
which is produced by Cheetah Television, part of Endemol UK plc.
Executive producers: Nikki Cheetham and Annette Clarke. Series editor: Jeremy Cross.

www.bbc.co.uk/restoration

Edited and brought to press by Adèle Campbell
Designed by Doug Cheeseman
Indexed by Alan Rutter
Printed by Bath Press c50, 7/06

Front cover: Corfe Castle, Dorset ©Andrew Ward/Getty Images
Photo of Ptolemy Dean courtesy of the Society for the Protection of Ancient Buildings

Contents

Endemol acknowledgements

Endemol would like to thank Jeremy Cross, Nikki Cheetham, Annette Clarke, Griff Rhys Jones, Ptolemy Dean, Marianne Sühr, Greg Stevenson, Roly Keating, Elaine Bedell, Andrea Miller, Audrey Baird, Sarah Barclay, Ian Lilley, Julian Thomas, Ian Scollay, Rhoni MacDonald, David Torbet, Kate Cotter, Charlotte Mackie, Louise Pirie, Gregor Myles, David Donald, Wendy Robertson, Ellie de Court, Andy Mackenzie, Susan King, Ian Tootle, Sandie Paterson, Neda Sharifi, Lucy Beveridge, Lloret Dunn, Katy Smith, Sarah McCabe, Charlie Gardner, Katie Nicholls, Rae Langford, Seema Khan, Sian Piddington, Philip Gulliver, Mark Balkham, Alasdair Glass, Ken Moth and Maggie Redfern.

The BBC would also like to thank Chris Arrowsmith, Kate Bradshaw, Richard Cable, Natalie Christian, Liz Cleaver, Samantha Durling, Ameneh Enayat, Craig Henderson, Jo Johnstone, Ian Lush, Hilda McLean, Rosemary Richards, Elizabeth Robertson and Darren Taylor.

Author's acknowledgements

Philip Wilkinson would like to thank: Adèle Campbell for her painstaking editorial management, Doug Cheeseman for his design, the team at Endemol for information and help and, for support in various ways, Zoë Brooks and Sugra Zaman.

The author would also like to extend special thanks to the following people – custodians, neighbours and supporters of the restoration candidates – for the help and information they have given him in the course of writing this book: Ross Aitken, Mark Bills, Mrs Black, Patrick Casement, Bill Chedham, Victoria Collison-Owen, Dominic Conway, Donna Corbin, Sam Cunningham, Rev Julyan Drew, Katy English, Matthew Gibb, Julian Goldie, Gill Green, David Gwyn, Fay Heard, Elaine Hughes, Perdita Hunt, David Johnston, Gwynne Jones, Les Jones, Graeme King, Susan McLean, Mo MacLeod, Jane Maskill, Judith Martin, Tim Meek, Rev Alan Megahey, John Miller, Billy Muir, Enid Mummery, Nigel Pink, Janice Planitzer, Helma Reynolds, John Southcote, Enid Stevenson and Nora Watson.

Foreword

by Ptolemy Dean

One might have hoped that after two series of *Restoration* all of the available derelict listed buildings would have been restored. Alas not. Perhaps, then, the public might have grown weary of the difficult and slow process of saving these old buildings? Happily, public interest appears to remain strong even though the number of forlorn and unloved structures remains tragically high. Part of this enthusiasm may come from an increasing awareness of the sustainability that recycling old buildings can offer. Why build something brand new if an old structure can be revived for a reduced energy cost? Another aspect is certainly an appreciation of the tremendous craftsmanship found in even the most humble of old buildings, which is lamentably all too often absent in the cost-governed quality of new work.

One senses in the building world that we are always being told we need to sweep away the out-dated and replace it with the new. The passage of time ensures that all things become 'out-dated' but this does not automatically mean they are no good. In a thoughtful and intelligent society old buildings can be adapted to serve current needs – this is, after all, what always happened in the parsimonious past. At the same time the process can encourage the revival of the craft and trade skills that are so desperately needed today. The presently fashionable rejection of the past, simply to make a political statement, is short sighted. I think we can 'modernise' and save our old buildings as well. Happily most people seem to agree, and for this reason: there may be some hope for our architectural heritage, whatever the official line of the government of the time.

This third series of *Restoration* had a new focus, on derelict structures within villages. As with previous series the buildings required a viable end use and a community who wished to see them 'restored'. How a 'village' might be defined is, needless to say, a matter of some debate. One building, Dennis Head Old Beacon on the Orkney isle of North Ronaldsay, commands a whole island of 66 souls to form a single scattered village. To the south of Scotland the former county court of Berwickshire finds itself not in a provincial capital, but at the heart of the former county town 'village' of Greenlaw. I have heard it said that the qualification for a village is a population of no more than 10,000 people. Whatever the population, *Restoration Village* immediately revealed the wonderfully rich variety of our rural settlements.

If one closes ones eyes to imagine what a typical village might look like, certain characteristic buildings immediately spring to mind. For me, the first one is an old parish church. It's a stone building, sitting in a graveyard and surrounded by a wall, and looks in part to be very old. Its tower rises above the village rooftops and can be seen from every angle; it would be unthinkable for it not to be there – and yet I am describing the old parish church of All Saints' at Beckingham in Lincolnshire, which is at risk through failed roofing and impending redundancy. If my church were harled and whitewashed I might be standing outside the equally vulnerable East Church at Cromarty in the Scottish Highlands. If it were of an early 19th-century date I could be describing the old estate church at Cushendun in Co Antrim, Northern Ireland. Village chapels are also at risk. Who could forget the enchanting and galleried interior of the disused Trinity Methodist Chapel in Newlyn, Cornwall? The way the old box pews appeared to cascade down the steeply raked galleries immediately reminds one of a stream gushing down a narrow Cornish valley.

And then there is the manor house. Most villages have one, yet sad and roofless is the venerable old pile of Pembrey Court, South Wales. I imagined how beautiful it could be partly restored, with the ruins of the outbuildings stabilised and kept as the framework for a beautiful garden. At Welcombe Barton, Devon, the old manor has just managed to keep its roof and is lovingly tended by volunteers as a retreat and escape from the

pressures of urban life. But it still needs help. Next in my dream village is the village institute, represented by a very generous and opulent Edwardian edifice in the small village of Newborough on Anglesey, north Wales. The unexpectedly metropolitan Prichard Jones Institute, with its rich panelling and stained-glass windows, was a gift to his home-town from one of the co-founders of the Dickens and Jones department store in London's Regent Street.

Villages have so frequently become dormitories for workers who commute to towns and cities elsewhere that it is easy to forget they once provided significant local employment. At the most basic level, most villages once possessed a forge and smithy. These serviced the local farm vehicles, carts and horses and were as indispensable as today's petrol stations. They were often accommodated in humble and unlisted shed-like structures which have become easy prey for new infill housing. At a village near Stratford upon Avon, Warwickshire, the old forge and carpentry works of Chedham's Yard has survived. The last family owner left in the 1970s, leaving the place exactly as it had been with tools, machines and general bits and pieces lying around. Old timber painted signs recalled an age when things were made locally by hand, and were repaired and maintained locally too – apparently the old carts used to queue down the lane awaiting attention. Whether such an extraordinary survival should be conserved as an historical artefact with all its atmospheric patina, or reconstructed as a facsimile for modern educational demonstrations, is a matter of some debate. At Dawe's Twine Works in West Coker, Somerset, a long, red pantiled roof meandering over a failing timber structure had managed to preserve evidence of a once-significant local industry that has all but disappeared.

Another major category of buildings in any village are the schools. The closure of these is always a matter of regret and the empty, silent and vandalised classrooms

at Gracehill's Old Primary School in Co Antrim, the one-time school at Massey's Folly in Upper Farringdon, Hampshire, and Pennoyer's School at Pulham St Mary in Norfolk, were sad and poignant places. The building at Gracehill was significant as it was an important component of the model village there, and its loss would leave a large and unwelcome hole. Pennoyer's School incorporated an ancient guild chapel and it was rather surprising to find its old west doorway concealed within a modern boiler-house addition. Elsewhere, layers of glossy institutional paint had failed to obliterate the unmistakable form of a medieval buttress. Massey's Folly in Upper Farringdon was a full-blown blood-red brick, late Victorian monster, the creation of a former vicar who built without architect's plans or any clear idea of what his building might be used for. Like all oddities the building should be preserved as an example of that splendid strain of eccentricity that sets these islands apart from everywhere else. Another undoubted eccentric was the late 19th-century painter G F Watts, whose gallery at Compton, Surrey, was built at his own expense to house his own work.

All of these buildings are vulnerable to decay and perhaps even eventual collapse. But one building seemed to summarise the fate of them all. Each day, the old timber granary and warehouse at Tollesbury, Essex, floods with the high tides. At these times the floorboards float upwards, only to be redeposited in roughly the same positions when the tide drops. With rising sea levels making the situation worse each year, it is the most graphic reminder that the reuse of our old buildings will not only revive our village communities, but will respond to our global responsibility to reuse and conserve.

Ptolemy Dean

Introduction

The first two series of *Restoration* captured the hearts and the minds of the nation. The first series, in summer 2003, has contributed significant funding towards the ongoing programme of restoration at the winning building, Manchester's magnificent early 20th-century Victoria Baths. The second series followed a year later and provided funding to restore the Old Grammar School and Saracen's Head in King's Norton on the edge of Birmingham. Now, two years after the last series was screened, *Restoration* is back once more – but this time with a change of perspective.

This time, the series is called *Restoration Village*, and its emphasis is on rural buildings. The series and this accompanying book examine a variety of fascinating buildings – as diverse as churches, galleries and mills – that are in or on the edge of villages and have the power, if restored, to bring huge benefits to their local communities.

In concentrating on rural buildings *Restoration Village* draws on an ancient tradition, because people in Britain have been gathering together and settling in villages for thousands of years. Villages go back to the Stone Age and there is a wonderfully preserved example at Skara Brae on Orkney, where a cluster of round stone houses retain many of their fixtures and fittings – stone cupboards, beds and hearths – still intact. There are traces of Bronze Age villages on Dartmoor and the earthworks left behind in the Iron Age, the period immediately before the Romans invaded, provide evidence of several kinds of rural settlement including the hillforts that sheltered village-like groups of houses, and small villages that probably survived through the Roman period.

Many of the villages we know today were probably established by Saxon times (the period

between the Roman withdrawal in the 5th century and the Norman invasion in 1066). Certainly thousands of village names are Saxon in origin. For example, those ending in '-ham' or '-ton' derive from Anglo-Saxon words for 'home' or 'farm', while those including the letters 'ing' refer to the family of a specific person.

In the centuries following the Saxon period many of the patterns of settlement that we still see today were mapped out in the form of roads, churches, houses and farms. These patterns were, and remain, fascinatingly varied. There are villages formed by a tight group of houses round a focal point such as a church or a road junction. There are long, straggling villages in which the houses are set on either side of a single street. There are villages arranged around a big central green. And there are endless variations, because most villages were not planned according to some preconceived formula but grew organically to suit specific needs.

If you fly over much of southern and eastern England it is easy to spot villages and they are remarkably evenly spread – usually a mile or so apart – across the landscape. In the north and west, especially in upland areas, villages are spread more sparsely and in many places the settlements consist of tiny hamlets and groups of farmsteads, but even here there are still villages aplenty.

In other parts of Britain the settlement pattern has its own variations. In Scotland, for example, the tightly knit or nucleated villages that are so common in England are less frequent, except south of the Firth of Forth. Further north Scotland has its own characteristic kind of rural settlement, the ferm-toun or clachan: a looser grouping of houses but one that still has the

> "With their ancient churches and timeless-looking cottages, many villages don't appear to have changed for centuries. But this is an illusion: villages have changed and are still evolving."

sense of community that distinguishes the village in all its forms.

So the vast majority of our villages are ancient places. The feature that marks them above all – their sense of community and local identity – is the result of centuries of history, demonstrated by the way, even today, many families can trace their roots in their local village back to the Victorian or Georgian periods, or even earlier still.

With their ancient churches and timeless-looking cottages, many villages don't appear to have changed for centuries. But this is usually an illusion: villages have changed a lot and are still evolving. And the changes themselves go back centuries. Most country walkers, for example, have come across bumps and depressions in fields that turn out to be the sole surviving remains of deserted villages, settlements that perished as long ago as the Middle Ages. Sometimes villages died out like this, but sometimes they moved to better land or a more convenient site and the earthworks are the evidence of the original site of a village that is now thriving down the road.

Developments such as these, with villages moving to new locations, go back at least to the Middle Ages. But there have also been more recent moves, including a number in the 18th century when rich landowners decided to remodel their country estates and demolished the local village to improve the view from their country house. It sounds brutal and often was, but sometimes the tenants benefited from new houses in a specially constructed 'model' estate village, a reminder that occasionally villages are planned from scratch.

The result of all these developments is a wonderful variety in the size and shape of rural settlements, most of which are home to close communities of people who like their village, want to go on living there and are committed to its cause. And there are rich architectural rewards to be found in our villages too. Although they are our smallest settlements, their range of building types and designs is enormous.

The houses alone are fascinating, especially the older ones built in the traditional style of their region, using locally sourced materials and techniques – from mud masonry to thatching – that have been honed and perfected over centuries. Then there are the churches, thousands of which were built before the Tudors came to the throne and the majority of which contain some beauty or interest that is hardly known outside their local region.

But this book shows that there is even more to our villages. Farm buildings, schools, lighthouses, follies, shops and ranges of industrial buildings, often small but frequently crucial to rural life, are a few of the structures that have emerged as restoration candidates. Some are extraordinary as architecture, some have long and absorbing histories, some are modest as buildings but have fascinating contents – but all have one thing in common: they are vital to their local community. Restoring them can make a huge difference, and their importance cannot be underestimated in this time of change in Britain's countryside.

Rural communities face huge challenges in the 21st century, many of which come from the difficulties caused by changes in the last few decades. One of the greatest challenges is posed by developments in agriculture. Many farmers, especially those with small farms, now find it hard to make a living from the land. There is a

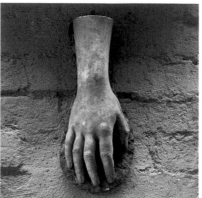

huge demand for cheap food but international competition means that much of this comes from overseas. Big buyers from the supermarket chains push down prices and European regulations mean that many farmers now make more money out of the subsidies they receive for looking after the rural landscape than from actually producing food. Some farmers have bucked this trend by selling directly to consumers through farmers' markets and farm shops, and by diversifying into unusual livestock and crops – from ostriches to new varieties of fruit. But for most farmers diversification is more likely to mean going into the bed-and-breakfast business or letting farm buildings to non-agricultural tenants.

The problems faced by farmers have an effect on farm buildings too. If a farmer no longer needs a barn – and in any case old barns are often unsuitable for modern farm machinery – the temptation may be to convert it into a luxury house, sell it and benefit from the booming property market. But many planners now turn down applications for such conversions because they usually involve major alterations to a historic building. Some kind of light industrial use – as a workshop for example – is more likely to preserve the historic structure of an old farm building. This is one example of how finding an appropriate new use can sometimes be the best solution to the problem of preserving an old building.

Farming is not the only rural industry to see decline, however, and many other country businesses and crafts have contracted or fallen by the wayside since the Second World War. Once every village had a blacksmith and a range of crafts were common in the countryside – from carpentry to pottery, basket-weaving to rope-making. Some of these, such as the specialised business of rope-making, once so important to the economy of some rural areas, have virtually disappeared; others have decamped to the bigger markets provided by the towns.

In some places rural crafts have been revived and many people are again experiencing the satisfaction that comes from making things by hand – for example with weaving, spinning or hurdle-making. And if some of this activity takes place in old rural buildings that were designed to house similar activities and processes, so much the better. Traditional building skills, from stoneworking to mud-masonry, are especially ripe for revival, and many UK heritage bodies are encouraging people to train in these skills and start careers in them.

One development that promises to put more money into the rural economy is the growth of home-working, whereby people work at home with an electronic link to a distant workplace. Ten years ago this was predicted to be the future of all kinds of work, office work especially. In practise many employers prefer to keep their employees on site where they can more easily be seen and supervised, but some businesses have taken to home-working. Their work, along with any high-tech businesses in rural areas, needs the right infrastructure, and computer-based businesses have been hampered in many rural areas by the lack of a broadband internet connection. Broadband has spread, but it is easy for city-dwellers to forget that many villages still don't have it (or cannot access the fastest broadband connection) and miss economic opportunities as a result. And it is likely that more redundant outbuildings and similar structures would be conserved and converted for work if broadband were available in more remote areas.

But bringing prosperity to impoverished areas is not simply a questioning of getting a faster internet connection. Not everyone is computer-literate after all, but even providing computer and internet training is not the answer. To succeed in the job market people need marketable skills, so training, technology and awareness of that market have to go hand in hand if opportunities are to be increased.

The lack of jobs has led to quite severe rural poverty in some areas. Cornwall, one of our most rural counties, is also one of our poorest – a fact that visitors can easily miss during the bustling holiday season. Because village populations are by definition quite small, rural poverty in general can be quite hard for outsiders to see or for politicians to deal with. The rural poor do not fill street upon street as they do in urban areas, but many villages contain a significant number of people who are unemployed, lack basic facilities or must stay close to home most of the time because they have no car.

Rural poverty is most evident in the housing market. Rural house prices now put many villages out of the reach of all but the well off, and people who grew up in a village very often cannot afford a house there. The price rises have been so steep that they now exclude lower-paid professionals such as teachers and nurses. Even rented accommodation is expensive and in most villages there is now very little social housing.

All this means there is an urgent requirement for affordable housing, housing that is within the reach of those in rural areas who have a real need. This in itself has implications for conservation, because those who care for our villages are often anxious that new houses will be out of place amongst more traditional countryside buildings.

But clearly they do not have to be. It is perfectly possible to design new houses using traditional materials that will fit into a village environment, provided that the will and the money are there. It is also sometimes possible to convert redundant buildings for residential use and satisfy both conservationists and prospective home-owners.

In spite of the hidden poverty, though, rural Britain is still for the most part a place where people want to live. For those who can afford it, a house in a village is often the ideal home, a place where they can enjoy the peace and scenery of the countryside and escape the hurly-burly of the city. But high property prices tend to weight the population of villages towards the rich and the elderly, and since those still in work mostly work outside the village, many villages are very quiet – often virtually empty – until the commuters come home in the evening. It is a far cry from the 'community' we imagine when we think of the traditional village.

A generally affluent population has its advantages of course. A village whose occupants have money to spend tends to have well-maintained houses and immaculate gardens, and many villages are now better kept than in the days when most of the cottages were owned by the local landlord and lived in by farm workers. But there are drawbacks too. When most people have a car they are more likely to travel to the local town to shop. Supermarkets provide competitive prices, plenty of choice and convenient parking, and as a result fewer and fewer villages have their own shops – most small village stores cannot survive on the villagers' odd purchases and a little passing trade. Similar economic pressures have forced the closure of many rural post offices too. A number of village pubs have also closed,

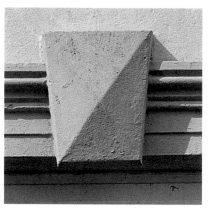

although pubs are on the whole better survivors, benefiting as they do from evening trade when the commuters come home as well as from people passing through during the day.

Over the last few years, however, some interesting enterprises have begun to take up part of the slack left by the demise of the village shop. More farmers sell from their own on-site shops and those who do so value the higher profits and the chance to learn directly from the consumer what people actually want. Other growers have begun 'vegetable box' schemes, delivering a weekly box of vegetables direct to people's doors. But the small shop and post office were buildings that were at the heart of many villages and their loss is deeply felt, especially by those who are less mobile.

And mobility is another key rural issue, as fewer and fewer villages are served by public transport. Bus companies on the whole only find it economic to run services between towns and the larger villages and the buses that do run are few and far between. So most country people find a car essential and those who cannot afford their own transport, or who cannot drive, have a difficult time. The young are a particular group who suffer because of the lack of public transport. Because of the population imbalance in many rural areas there are fewer young people in villages anyway – hundreds of village schools have closed because there are too few children to justify keeping them going. The young people who remain find they have little to do and it is hard for them to get to the towns to visit friends or go to the cinema. The happiest communities, by contrast, are those that include the young in their planning – and that goes for towns and villages alike.

Although there are undoubtedly many problems facing villages today, village communities are nevertheless generating countless initiatives to improve life. From local rural broadband schemes to enlightened conversions of farm buildings, from farm shops to car-sharing groups, from evening classes to community-run pubs, villages are finding ways of facing the challenges of 21st-century rural life. When these activities take place in a restored historic building there is a conservation gain to set alongside the social benefit. Villages are adapting, as they always have.

Restoring a building is one form of adaptation that can have a huge impact, especially on a small community. A restoration can create a public space that local people can use, provide a space for information displays about the history of both building and village, develop a visitor attraction that will bring people in and encourage them to spend money locally and can lead to the start of new businesses, creating jobs and generating income. Groups who can benefit range from schools to local history societies, but in most cases the whole village has something to gain, because even a small project such as a restored shop or barn can transform a small place.

The buildings in *Restoration Village* are all different. They pose all kinds of challenges – to planners, craftworkers and fundraisers alike. And all such projects are unique, not just because of the differences between the buildings but because the needs of local communities are endlessly varied too. We can all learn from these projects, taking away a sense of the importance of buildings to people and of the immense potential that buildings can realise. These visionary projects should inspire many more. ▪

Site Map

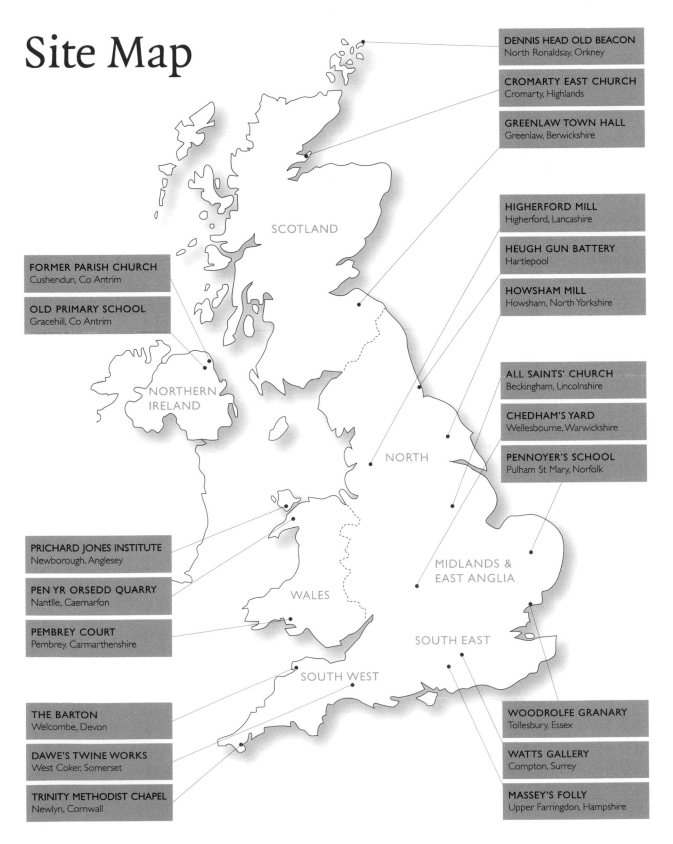

DENNIS HEAD OLD BEACON
North Ronaldsay, Orkney

CROMARTY EAST CHURCH
Cromarty, Highlands

GREENLAW TOWN HALL
Greenlaw, Berwickshire

HIGHERFORD MILL
Higherford, Lancashire

HEUGH GUN BATTERY
Hartlepool

HOWSHAM MILL
Howsham, North Yorkshire

ALL SAINTS' CHURCH
Beckingham, Lincolnshire

CHEDHAM'S YARD
Wellesbourne, Warwickshire

PENNOYER'S SCHOOL
Pulham St Mary, Norfolk

FORMER PARISH CHURCH
Cushendun, Co Antrim

OLD PRIMARY SCHOOL
Gracehill, Co Antrim

PRICHARD JONES INSTITUTE
Newborough, Anglesey

PEN YR ORSEDD QUARRY
Nantlle, Caernarfon

PEMBREY COURT
Pembrey, Carmarthenshire

THE BARTON
Welcombe, Devon

DAWE'S TWINE WORKS
West Coker, Somerset

TRINITY METHODIST CHAPEL
Newlyn, Cornwall

WOODROLFE GRANARY
Tollesbury, Essex

WATTS GALLERY
Compton, Surrey

MASSEY'S FOLLY
Upper Farringdon, Hampshire

SCOTLAND

NORTHERN IRELAND

NORTH

WALES

MIDLANDS & EAST ANGLIA

SOUTH EAST

SOUTH WEST

South West

T he South West is one of the most rural of the English regions. There are few big towns and only two really large cities – Plymouth and Bristol – so many of the area's people live in villages or small towns and these settlements have a strong local character.

Nowhere is far from the coast in the South West and much of its character has to do with the region's close links to the sea; links that are embodied in the region's restoration candidates. Trinity Methodist Chapel in Newlyn is a monument to the importance of religious nonconformity in the lives of people involved in the fishing industry – not just the fishermen themselves but many of those involved in selling the catch and working in allied businesses and

crafts too. Dawe's Twine Works at West Coker is in an inland village but one connected by an umbilical road link to coastal Bridport – a place where rope, twine and sailcloth were much in demand. The Barton at Welcombe is a cluster of farm buildings just a short walk from the coast and within earshot of smuggling tales. The stunning, rocky coast of the South West is a key element in the stories of these places and of the character of the region as a whole.

This character is easy to recognise: Cornwall, for example, has local distinctiveness in spades. Say 'Cornwall' and most people think of fishing villages with narrow roads and alleys full of tightly packed houses, mostly built of stone but rendered and whitewashed to protect them from

DAWE'S TWINE WORKS
West Coker, Somerset

TRINITY METHODIST CHAPEL
Newlyn, Cornwall

the coast's battering storms. They have slate roofs and even these are often rendered to keep out the driving rain and salty sea spray. Cornwall's main building stone is granite and in inland areas there are still many farms and village houses in which this grey stone is left bare.

There is granite in Devon too – on Dartmoor – but much of Devon's geology is made up of sandstone and clay. This clay was one Devon's most popular building materials; mixed with straw it was used unbaked to make cob, Devon's traditional walling material. Cob walls often curve organically and are protected by deeply overhanging thatched roofs.

The rest of the South West benefits from all sorts of different local building stones. To journey through the region is to experience a constantly changing rural scene, with buildings of blue lias and golden limestone in parts of Somerset, limestone again in Gloucestershire, greensand and grey sarsen (the material of the large stones at Stonehenge) in areas of Wiltshire, and flint (often in combination with brick or other materials) in Dorset. This variety of stones and building techniques, together with outstanding scenery both on the coast and inland, make the South West a region of great beauty.

But these buildings are more than just scenery. They were built by real people, responding to real human needs – the needs of fishermen in Cornwall, dairy farmers in Somerset and their colleagues in a range of rural industries. And these human needs do not go away. Look beyond the picturesque beauty of the Cornish fishing village, Devon's lanes and the rolling hills of Somerset, and you will find rural economies trying hard to change with the times. In some areas it is especially hard: Cornwall, for example, is one of the poorest English counties.

Traditionally, people in the South West have more often than not made their living from two main industries – fishing and farming – or from trades linked to these businesses. Both fishing and farming are now facing difficulties. Fishing used to be the mainstay of the Cornish economy with fleets in practically every coastal village. There were fishing ports on the Devon and Dorset coasts too. Now, although the industry is still strong in one or two ports – Newlyn and Brixham for example – it is far from the big business it once was. Hampered by an ageing fleet it has to face up to challenges such as foreign competition and ever-changing food fashions, and needs to find new markets for the catch.

And as fishing has become less profitable so too have its allied industries, such as fish processing, marketing and selling. One challenge is to keep these near the ports so that Cornwall can benefit from all the income that comes from the sea.

Agriculture is still a major earner in the region. The South West is home to one quarter of the national dairy stock and there are substantial numbers of pigs and beef-cattle. But farming has been beset by uncertainties in recent years and the recent outbreaks of BSE and foot-and-mouth disease both hit the South West. And the ever-changing demands of everyone from European policy-makers to supermarket buyers give farmers very little room to manoeuvre, and very little profit at the end of the year.

There is a glimmer of hope in the shape of a movement to concentrate on quality, for example by using the South West's lush grass to produce fine beef and Dorset lamb. And local development agencies are playing their part, helping to grow new skills in the fields and new markets beyond the farm gate. But it is an uphill struggle, for farmer and worker alike.

Industry provides one answer and the South West has both high-tech businesses and a strong marine sector. Tourism has helped the region too, channelling in money and bringing new life to old fishing villages. But this industry too has suffered, with foot-and-mouth disease keeping visitors away and cheap air travel taking more and more of them overseas each year anyway. And even in the best of times tourism is a seasonal business –

Left Cobbles at Welcombe Barton: there may be other cobbled floors hidden beneath later surfaces in some of the farm's buildings.

Below left At Dawe's Twine Works many items used in the twine-making business, such as these spools, are preserved.

Below A pair of mallets commemorate the construction of the Sunday School at Newlyn's Trinity Chapel.

though the Eden Project, the South West's biggest visitor attraction, has bucked this trend and attracts millions of visitors all year round.

But important as Eden is, it is only one attraction. The region needs, and is beginning to get, better overall strategies to attract people outside of the summer months and more targeted publicity and marketing offer further hope. The region's exceptional beauty make it likely that visitor numbers will grow.

This is one important area in which the restoration of old buildings can help; historic buildings are an intrinsic part of the character of the South West. Whether sites like Welcombe Barton, West Coker's Twine Works and Newlyn's Trinity Methodist Chapel become visitor attractions or not, their restoration will add greatly to the life of their villages and to our knowledge of their history. For these reasons alone they are worth restoring. ▪

The Barton
Welcombe, Devon

> "Old farmhouses like Welcombe Barton are apt to draw such myths around them. But most of their history was probably one of hard work for low returns."

For thousands of years the countryside of Britain has been shaped by the activities of farmers. The pattern of fields and hedgerows, and every kind of structure from gates to field barns to cottages, all are there because of their practical role in this most vital of activities. Many look as if they have existed, apparently unchanged, for centuries. But in fact agriculture is evolving all the time, adapting to changing needs and markets. Farms evolve too, acquiring extra barns and extensions as the need arises. But sometimes farm buildings, and even entire farms, get stranded in the process of change.

The Barton, often referred to as Welcombe Barton, was one such farm in crisis. A group of buildings dating back to at least the 17th century – and probably to the Middle Ages – the farm saw a period of decline in the 20th century before it was donated to the Yarner Trust, which runs courses in ecology, agriculture, sustainable living and conservation. Now, although the building is in need of restoration, it is the base of a thriving charity. It is also at the heart of a close and supportive local community, as Jane Maskill, Adminstrator to the Yarner Trust, explains: 'Welcombe is a rather scattered village, made up of a number of separate hamlets. But it is a close

Opposite A cluster of stone buildings next to the house forms a backdrop for the work of gardener and basket-weaver.

Above This delightful touch, a terracotta head surrounded by green leaves, embodies the link between people and environment espoused by the Yarner Trust.

Above A section of cob walling abuts stone masonry; both are local materials that Devon builders handled instinctively.

Opposite One of the buildings at Welcombe that has already been restored shows the commitment of the Yarner Trust to maintaining the site to the highest standards.

parish, probably going back to the Middle Ages.

The medieval period was a time of change for many rural communities in Cornwall and Devon. The move from big open fields to the more familiar patchwork of smaller fields that we know today came in the 18th century in many parts of England. But here it happened much earlier, beginning back in the 13th century and virtually complete by the end of the 15th. By then there was certainly a house at Welcombe Barton, perhaps home to a farmer growing crops and raising pigs and sheep.

By the 17th century this farmer was probably doing rather well, judging from the buildings on the site that date from this period. What survives is a stone farmhouse together with various outbuildings – including a bakehouse, pigsty and barn.

These buildings are typical country structures put up using local materials and labour, without the services of an architect, to suit the user's needs. The house and much of the main outbuilding, the barn, are built of sandstone rubble, the main stone-walling material used in Devon and the Cornish borders. It gives the walls a pleasing pinkish-grey tinge that looks well beneath the slate roof. Another type of building material probably used were cobbles, which would have been used for the floors of the outbuildings and the adjoining yards. Some of these may remain beneath the more recent floors of earth or concrete.

Part of the barn is walled in another typical Devon material, cob. A cob wall is basically made of mud, but building it was not as simple as that makes it sound. First you had to mix the mud with other ingredients to bind it and make it strong. Straw was always added and sometimes fragments of waste slate were included for extra strength. The mix was treaded – either by horses, oxen or the builders themselves – and then the cob was formed into lumps and added to the wall in layers. Each layer was about a foot high and when complete was left to dry, sometimes for a week or two, before the next one was added.

Cob walls were always thick – usually two feet or more – and were generally coated with a layer of plaster or limewash to keep out the moisture. The walls usually stood on a plinth of stone or pebbles to deter rising damp and were topped with a generously overhanging roof to keep off the rain. With this protection – what Devon

and helpful community. For example, when the local pub had been empty for about three years, 30 or 40 people volunteered to clean it up and make it ready for the new licensee. It's the same when the village hall grass needs cutting – everyone turns up with their lawnmowers.'

The place that this community calls home is in the extreme north-west part of Devon near the border with Cornwall; a quiet and idyllic corner of England that is also part of the North Devon Area of Outstanding Natural Beauty. The settlement, of Tudor cottages and small Georgian houses, sits amongst wooded valleys and fields. The people who live here either commute to neighbouring towns, work on the land, or work from home running holiday accommodation, the local pub, or the pottery. Welcombe Barton itself has evolved as a result of centuries of farming activity in the builders called 'a good hat and a good pair of shoes' – a cob wall could last for centuries.

Most of the outbuildings at Welcombe Barton probably originally had thatched roofs – cob and thatch is a traditional Devon combination. But this would have changed in the 19th century when slate became increasingly popular for roofing. Slate was, in fact, virtually a local material, having been common in Cornwall for centuries. But the revolution in slate roofs came with the opening up of slate mines in Wales and the improvements in transport brought by the railways. By Queen Victoria's reign houses with Welsh slate roofs were being built everywhere from Middlesbrough to Middlesex, and on farm buildings in Devon too. Later still came corrugated iron, which farmers valued because it was cheap, waterproof and easy for unskilled workers to fit; Welcombe Barton, like virtually every farm, has its share.

By the time of the Welsh slate boom, in 1842, Welcombe Barton was owned by the Rev Peter Glubb and leased to one William Tremur. So it's possible that by this time it was a glebe farm, in other words one that had been given by the lord of the manor to the church – perhaps when Welcombe became a parish in 1530.

This association with the church links the farm to one of the most famous local characters of the time, the vicar of Welcombe and nearby Morwenstow, Robert Stephen Hawker. Hawker was one of the great 19th-century eccentrics. Ministering to a population of fishermen, farmers, smugglers and wreckers in his remote coastal parish, Hawker was adamant that men drowned at sea should whenever possible receive a decent Christian funeral. Sometimes he was seen scrambling down the cliffs to retrieve bodies and take them to the churchyard for burial. He was vicar of Morwenstow for just over 40 years and for much of this time also looked after the neighbouring parish of Welcombe.

Hawker was also a prolific writer, often to be found sitting in his driftwood hut smoking opium, admiring the view along the coast to Tintagel and writing about the Cornwall he loved so much. He specialised in accounts of famous Cornish people and popular poems about Cornwall and its history.

From his motley parishioners, Hawker no doubt learned much about notorious coastal pastimes such as smuggling. He also researched stories about infamous local characters and

Village Voice

"These are just great buildings that could really do with a lift and with an investment they could be here for a long time. They're our future and it's a place that we would like to leave for other people. The help that people could give us on this, to keep it here for future generations, would be just wonderful."

JANE MASKILL Welcombe Barton

turned them into poems. One example was John – or Jan – Coppinger, reputedly a seaman from Denmark who was washed up on shore, abducted local girl Dinah Hamlyn, and embarked on a career of piracy along the Cornish coast. He is supposed to have amassed a great fortune and hidden it in a cave and in a farm that he bought in the area – perhaps a more remote farm than Welcombe Barton but no doubt one with equally suitable barns in which to stash booty.

The truth was more prosaic. The real Coppinger, Daniel Herbert Coppinger, was wrecked at Welcombe Mouth in 1792 and was probably an Irishman. He did marry (but did not abduct) a Miss Hamlyn, became involved in smuggling and was last heard of as a bankrupt in the King's Bench Prison in London. For Hawker, though, Coppinger was a romantic figure of myth and mystery:

> Will you hear of Cruel Coppinger
> He came from a foreign land;
> He was brought to us by salt water,
> He was carried away by the wind.

The most famous of Hawker's poems, *Song of the Western Men*, was a ballad celebrating Jonathan Trelawny, one of several 17th-century bishops imprisoned in the Tower of London for refusing to agree to one of King James II's policies of tolerance towards Catholics and Dissenters. Trelawny, supported by his fellow Cornishmen, was acquitted. The refrain of Hawker's ballad – 'And shall Trelawny die? Here's twenty thousand Cornishmen Will know the reason why!' – became a sort of unofficial Cornish national anthem. (Some think the poem is not by Hawker at all: it was originally published anonymously and Hawker only claimed it for one of his own some years afterwards. Locals held that part of it at least was drawn from a much older ballad.)

Old farmhouses like Welcombe Barton are apt to attract such myths. But most of their history was probably one of hard work for low returns. This area of the West Country hardly boomed through the last 200 years. In 1801 there were 220 people in Welcombe village, a figure that rose to 292 in 1841 but fell steadily to just 117 in 1961, though rallying slightly to 170 in 2001.

The declining population paralleled a decline in farming. In 1871, twenty or so local men were farmers and a slightly larger number were farm labourers. Today, there are still about 30 families involved in agriculture in some way, but probably

Top A deep fireplace and stone-flagged floor make an inviting interior in the farmhouse.

Above Natural wood and stone surfaces complement the restored interiors.

only half of their members work on the land. Meanwhile, many of the cottages once occupied by farm labourers are now home to retired people or are used for holiday accommodation.

Welcome Barton itself survived the change of use that came about when the property was donated to the Yarner Trust in 1979; it is a good fit of building and function. Jane Maskill puts it like this: 'When I get there in the morning it doesn't feel like coming to work, and it feels right that this old building should still be used for activities that are based around the land and the environment.' People come from all over the country to take part in a range of courses, including some that teach the craft and conservation skills used in the restoration of old buildings. The farm also hosts several local groups, who share their skills in crafts such as spinning, weaving and dying, embroidery and patchwork and willow weaving.

Now is the time, before the building deteriorates too drastically, to do the necessary repairs and to give the farm a new and fuller life at the centre of the community. The Yarner Trust has already made a start. Its members have just completed restoration work on the bakehouse, which was on the point of collapsing, with the help of a grant of £45,000 from the Heritage Lottery Fund. As Jane Maskill explains, they now hope to restore the whole complex in order to bring other rooms into full use: 'Making more rooms and buildings available will enable us to use specific parts of the farm for specific activities. It will also provide the opportunity to make the buildings fully accessible for people with disabilities.' A complete restoration scheme could give the Yarner Trust a lasting base and benefit the local community, as well as giving back to Devon one of its most charming and typical buildings. ■

Below A tiny window sits in a deep opening, showing the thickness of Welcombe Barton's walls. The opening is slightly splayed, with the effect that the window lets in more light than one expects for such a small area of glass.

Dawe's Twine Works
West Coker, Somerset

> "Twine was being made there by 1830, and the history of the industry in West Coker may go back even further."

Rope, string and twine were once part of all our lives. Farmers bound bundles of corn together with twine, parcels were tied with it, it was wound around the handles of tools and virtually anything could be mended with it. Rope was used wherever heavy loads were hauled or lifted and was essential, of course, on sailing ships. Before the invention of man-made fibres in the 20th century all this rope and twine was manufactured from natural materials such as flax or hemp and, since the product was put under constant strain and often broke, there was always a demand for more. So rope and twine were made everywhere, especially in places close to the sea.

One area with a particular speciality in rope- and twine-making was Somerset, where conditions were just right for growing the raw materials required. Around 30 twine works are recorded in Somerset in the 19th century and Dawe's Twine Works, in the village of West Coker near Yeovil, is one of the few survivors. Twine was being made there by 1830 and the history of the industry in West Coker may go back even further.

Ross Aitken, parish councillor and acting Chairman of the Coker Rope and Sail Trust, explains the local importance of the business: 'This industry was crucial to the whole history of the area. Everyone was involved in some way in the business of growing hemp and flax or processing it to make rope or cloth. So there were once lots of rope works, but they quietly died out when the demand disappeared and now there are very few left.' So, strange as it seems to modern eyes, manufacturing industry was at the heart of this picturesque Somerset village in countryside reached by narrow lanes cut deep into the local sandstone. In the 19th century it seemed

as natural as the flax growing in the fields.

Twine works and roperies are simple working buildings but they have one striking feature: their length. They are long, narrow buildings rather like corridors leading nowhere; no other structures are quite like them. But there is a good reason for their odd shape as these buildings are perfectly designed for the process they housed. Twine was produced by twisting several threads together and an important part of the production process involved 'walking' the twine from one end of the long building to the other. The main building, or twine walk, at West Coker is 100 yards (91m) long.

At one end of the walk was a spinning wheel, which would originally have been turned by hand. The man who was producing the twine carried a bundle of hemp fibres around his waist.

He drew some fibres from the bundle and attached them to a hook on the wheel. As the wheel turned the worker walked backwards, feeding out more fibres from the bundle as he went. The quality of the yarn produced was down to the skill of the backwards-walking worker in teasing out just the right amount.

This process resulted in lengths of thread that would be twisted together to form twine. The twine was washed by soaking in tanks of water before being stretched out along the twine walk, polished with horsehair, and stretched again. In the early days the processes of walking and twisting the twine were done by hand but later machinery was devised to do the job.

The twine walk at Dawe's is a typically long and narrow structure made of simple wooden frames bolted together. On top is a roof of double

Opposite Heavy clay tiles are making their weight felt on the twine walk's roof timbers, with the result that the structure has distorted well out of true.

Above The roof timbers of the twine walk give just enough headroom for a worker to 'walk the twine'. When the building was in use there would have been much less of the fascinating industrial clutter that survives there today.

Roman tiles, a form of traditional clay roof-tile with two waterways. The examples at West Coker were made by A G Pitts at Highbridge, the area of North Somerset where there is plentiful clay and a tradition of brick- and tile-making. Inside are two floors: an upper floor or loft where the twine was walked and a ground floor where it was finished. There is not much more to the building. Though parts of it are boarded off to provide some shelter to the workers, much of the structure is open-sided to provide good ventilation. The wooden uprights of the timber frame stand on the earth floor. It is as simple as that.

In the yard next to the twine walk are several other buildings. A brick-built engine room and coal store point to the fact that there was once a steam engine on the site to power the machinery. The engine itself has long gone but there is a concrete base that supported its successor, an oil engine; later still there was an electric motor. Other buildings in the yard include a workshop. Known simply as 'the shop', this is built of brick and is above a water tank, suggesting that it was used for processes such as 'retting' (soaking) hemp or flax and washing twine.

Altogether it makes a modest complex of buildings, but one with a big story to tell about an industry that made up a huge part of Somerset's economy in the 19th century. Other parts of the local scene show the marks of this once-important business too. A nearby hill has steps cut into its slope to make terraces where rope and twine could be left to dry. The village itself preserves retting ponds, where flax was soaked, and the Booking House Stalls where twine, and

perhaps sailcloth, were sold. Hemp tended to be a small-scale crop, popular amongst cottagers who used it to supplement their income. Flax, in widespread demand for the manufacture of linen as well as twine, was grown on a larger scale by farmers who often incorporated it into crop rotations with turnips, wheat and barley.

Indeed, rope and twine were being made in these parts for centuries before the structures at West Coker were built. Records certainly show that flax was being grown at Rimpton, north-east of Yeovil, in 1264–5. The West Coker tithe records mention hemp in 1309 and in the mid-14th century yarn from Coker was being sent to Bridport on the Dorset coast, suggesting an early link with ships and the sea.

By the 17th century the Yeovil area was a major centre for the cultivation of flax and hemp, but in the 18th century the authorities actually had to encourage farmers and growers to produce the plants by offering a special bounty. Many applications for bounties came from the Coker area, suggesting that flax and hemp cultivation survived here and continued into the following century too. It is said that by this time West Coker had no fewer than five rope or twine walks and that every house had a loom for the production of cloth. The industry was at the very heart of the life and economy of the village.

The payment of the bounty, the exports to Bridport and the production of sailcloth and ropes point to the enormous significance of this trade. In the centuries before air travel Britain's security depended on its navy, and the ships needed both sails and ropes. West Coker is an

Opposite Some of the outer walls consist of wooden boards nailed to the structural framework, and these have been patched in places with sheets of corrugated iron.

Below All kinds of twine-making machinery jostles for attention, while in the background workers' scribbled notes remain on the boards that make up the walls.

Above Tangles of rope and twine, like these on the old clerk's desk, have remained since the business closed in the 1960s.

Below The lower floor of the twine walk is open-sided, for maximum ventilation.

went out across the Atlantic to fish for cod off Newfoundland. From there they sailed to the Caribbean where they sold some of the cod, taking local rum on board. Then they crossed the Atlantic again, selling the rest of their catch in the Catholic states of southern Europe before returning to England with the rum. It's extraordinary to think these tiny boats made such a long journey.'

Those on board must have been remarkable sailors and the region certainly had at least one famous maritime son. William Dampier (1652–1715), navigator and privateer, was born in neighbouring East Coker. Dampier led several long-distance expeditions, becoming the first person to sail around the world twice. He visited the Philippines, China and Australia on one voyage and explored Australia's west coast on another. He gave his name to the Dampier Archipelago and Strait, published accounts of his voyages, and was an associate of Alexander Selkirk, the inspiration for Daniel Defoe's *Robinson Crusoe*.

inland village but is still little more than 12 miles (19km) from the sea. Its people must have felt a strong connection with maritime life and a real sense of the part local rope and cloth played in Britain's seafaring history – whether our sailors were defending the coastline, engaged in overseas conquest, or embarking on journeys of exploration, their ships needed West Coker's products.

Ross Aitken stresses the international significance of the trade: 'Going back to the 17th and 18th centuries, small boats from this area

The fact that Dampier was a privateer – a kind of licensed pirate – lends credence to the stories of smuggling and shady dealing that are told about the Coker area. There was certainly plenty of trade between Coker and the coast, and some of it involved illicit brandy and other products brought in 'through the back door'.

But much of Coker's business was more

Village Voice

"It means an enormous amount to the village because it's the history of what we did. So many of the people really want to help with it, and to use their expertise in putting it back together again."

ROSS AITKEN West Coker

legitimate. Sailcloth, made especially in East Coker and Crewkerne, was one of the region's most important products, one that sat comfortably beside the rope and twine also used by the navy. One Crewkerne company, Hayward's, made the sailcloth used on Nelson's flagship, HMS *Victory*. So this quiet part of rural Somerset played its part in one of the most famous moments in British maritime history.

Dawe's Twine Works has its own place in this history, since the making of twine was an integral part of the sail-making industry. A manufacturer called Israel Rendell was a twine-maker on the site from 1830 until 1875. He sold the business on to the Gould family and a couple of years later (probably in 1877) it passed to John William Dawe, who was listed as a twine-maker at the 'Millbrook Works', named after the adjacent family residence, Millbrook House. Rendell may well have made his twine in the open air, in the old-fashioned way. It was probably Dawe who put the process under cover by building the twine walk that survives today, since the structure first appears on the large-scale Ordnance Survey map in 1903.

The business remained in the hands of the Dawe family until it closed in 1968, by which time

the use of modern packaging materials such as adhesive tape had caused the demand for twine to plummet. But the building was untouched and, thanks in part to the Somerset Industrial Archaeology Society, the twine-making machinery is still in situ.

The twine walk building is now at risk, mainly because the weight of its roof tiles is proving too much for the wooden structure. Much of it is now supported by scaffolding but it has survived – just – and could be the heart of an absorbing heritage project. The buildings could become a base for a display of the twine-making machinery, for information about this industry and for oral history work. A restoration along these lines would provide a real boost to West Coker, and as Ross Aitken points out: 'Local people are really committed to this project. There are still strong memories of the twine works and people are eager to see it restored.' Many of those who live in the area now work in Yeovil but the village has always been a working community and locals are keen for the area to be one in which people both live and work. As well as creating jobs, the whole site could provide a fascinating insight into a once-important industry that gave rural Somerset a vital place in Britain's seafaring past. ■

Trinity Methodist Chapel
Newlyn, Cornwall

"The miners and fisherman of Cornwall knew about danger. They risked their skins, down the pit or on the sea, every day of their lives."

Methodist chapels are easy to overlook. They do not have tall towers like many Anglican parish churches, they do not advertise themselves with garish signs like shops or pubs and, in contrast to many industrial buildings, they usually blend into their surroundings. But these unassuming buildings have played a huge part in people's lives. In Cornwall especially, where there are still more than 550 Methodist chapels, they are found in towns and villages across the country.

The Methodist movement began in the mid-18th century when two Anglican preachers, the brothers John and Charles Wesley, began to invigorate the Church of England with a message of faith, repentance and a more disciplined religious life. Their message found huge appeal, though not within the hierarchy of the Church of England, and by the 1790s the Methodists had gone their own way and the movement continued to expand rapidly though the 19th century.

Cornwall was one of the places where the new faith proved especially popular. John Wesley preached to thousands at open-air meetings and travelling preachers quickly spread the word across the county. Their message was simple: live according to the 'method' laid down in the Bible, have faith in Jesus Christ as your saviour, and you will achieve salvation.

This message proved attractive to many Cornish men and women. The miners and fisherman of Cornwall knew a lot about danger: they risked their skins, down the pit or on the sea, every day of their working lives. A religious message delivered with directness, often in the dialect spoken by ordinary people and offering a clear route to salvation, had an obvious appeal. Travelling preachers spread the word from place to place, holding religious meetings out of doors or in people's homes, and the new faith soon began to take root in Cornwall.

Before the 18th century was over Methodist chapels were springing up all over the county and Newlyn was no exception. In far western Cornwall, on the coast near Penzance, it is famous for its harbour – a deep-water anchorage

Opposite A view of the chapel's gallery shows how the pews are packed densely in, to accommodate the largest possible congregation in the available space.

Below Newlyn has one of Cornwall's few fishing harbours that is still busy.

Village Voice

"Well I think it is lovely to think it is going to be preserved because, as I say, the chapel has been used for two centuries now, and we have such happy memories of being here. It's the closeness of the people that are here – we're all friends together, and everyone helps everyone out. And I think that is one of the nicest things of being associated with Trinity."

ENID STEVENSON Newlyn

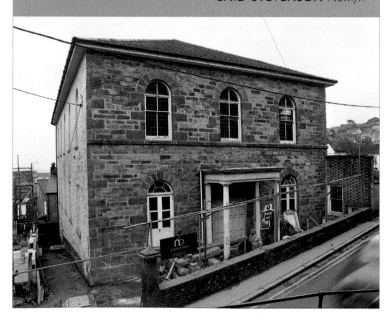

shielded from the prevailing west and south-west winds, which has been sheltering fishing boats since the Middle Ages. The harbour covers some 40 acres and the busy fish market attracts buyers from Europe as well as from the local area. Its fleet, sizeable for centuries, still boasts almost 200 vessels. Newlyn has been a thriving fishing centre for more than 500 years and by the 19th century was home to people involved in a host of dependent businesses, such as fish merchants, shipwrights, barrel-makers and chandlers.

The congregation at Newlyn's Trinity Chapel was of Wesleyan Methodists. Distinct from the Primitive Methodists – who attracted mainly members of the working class such as fishermen – the Wesleyans probably included many of Newlyn's merchants and craft workers. They were prosperous as well as religious and wanted a building that was worthy of their social status and their faith.

The foundation stone of their chapel was laid on 27 January 1834. This would have been the culmination of a long period of planning and fund-raising, during which time the Wesleyans must have worshipped at another, simpler building, perhaps on the same site. They would have held many bazaars, events at which anything and everything – craft goods, fruit, vegetables, agricultural produce, and hundreds of raffle tickets – was sold to raise money for the church. These bazaars often had a theme, with some places having Shakespearean, Grecian or Egyptian bazaars, decorated with hired theatrical scenery. The result would have been an entertaining afternoon out for locals, and more money in the bank to fund the building programme.

No-one knows who designed Trinity Chapel, but the people of Newlyn probably did so without an architect. It was quite normal for local builders or masons to design buildings such as chapels, following the specifications of the minister. To produce the details builders referred to pattern books, which contained engravings of doorways, windows, mouldings and other details ready for copying.

The process of fundraising and designing must have been successful for the Newlyn Wesleyans because the chapel opened on 20 March 1835 – little more than a year after the foundation stone was laid. It was a handsome building, with solid walls of local granite, a big

Gothic window and twin entrance doors facing the street. Newlyn prospered throughout the 19th century and the Methodists upgraded their chapel several times. It was extended in 1866, a large pulpit was provided, and an organ was bought and installed in 1875. The Rev Julyan Drew emphasises the fact that this is a chapel that has developed over the years: 'This is a building that has evolved as time has gone by. Many of the interior features, such as the pulpit, were added decades after the chapel was built. Other fittings, like the communion rails, have been moved.' So the building that survives is the fruit of decades of Methodist enthusiasm and prosperity through the Victorian period.

In spite of its rather large Gothic window, Trinity Methodist Chapel does not look very spectacular from the outside. But the interior is a different story, an object lesson in 19th-century chapel decoration and furnishing. There is a sweeping, horseshoe-shaped gallery, a fine collection of box pews and a big pulpit, centrally placed. The whole space is designed to accommodate the maximum number of people within hearing-distance of the pulpit, for what mattered here was that everyone could hear the word of God preached.

It was important for people to be able to see clearly too, so that they could read their hymn books and perhaps follow a reading in their Bible. So, unlike many Anglican and Catholic churches, chapels like Trinity generally had clear glass in the windows; the stained glass at Newlyn is a later addition. But even with this change the chapel's interior is little short of perfect – a testimony to those who worked so hard to build and maintain it over the years.

Through the 19th century the chapel's congregation probably increased in number and prosperity, as Newlyn's fishing industry went from strength to strength. Mackerel, pilchard and herring were the staple fish, with impressive catches throughout the Victorian period. Today more exotic species are caught, such as monkfish and John Dory, as well as the more familiar mackerel.

But this prosperity never came easily. For one thing, fishing is a dangerous business and rough seas always took their toll. For another, fishermen sometimes had to fight for their fishing rights. The most famous example is the Newlyn riots, which broke out in 1896 during a dispute between local fishermen and those from England's east coast, who also used Newlyn harbour. Religion played its part in the tension between the two groups, because the east-coast fishermen were prepared to go to sea on Sundays while the fishermen of Newlyn refused to break the Sabbath. In addition, east-coast catches often came in more quickly and were sold before the fish from the Newlyn boats, depriving locals of their income. On Monday 18 May the dispute

Above left A stained-glass window in the gallery glows with colour; the image illustrates the text, 'Blessed are the pure in heart'.

Above right Simple capital-letter forms are used for these signs on the gallery doors.

Opposite The chapel's plain entrance, with Classical porch and round-topped windows, opens onto a busy road.

came to a violent climax. Newlyn protesters boarded east-coast boats and threw their catches into the harbour. Over the next couple of days the conflict raged on, with a hut belonging to a Lowestoft agent burned down, fist-fights in local pubs, a pitched battle between the two sides and, finally, the intervention of the army. The bayonets and swords of the troops proved too much for the rioters and peace was eventually restored.

In spite of the involvement of large crowds in the riots, only eight men were charged and none was given a prison sentence. They came back home to Newlyn as heroes and were welcomed with flags, candles and stirring music from the local band. They were triumphant – but also thoughtful. They knew in their hearts that if their industry was to survive it would have to adapt. Younger men realised they would have to go to sea on Sundays. They would also have to be more commercially alert, more open to change and more aware of markets for different kinds of fish. In this they succeeded, and Newlyn continued to prosper as one of the country's most productive fishing ports.

Newlyn was changing in other ways, too. By the 1880s it had become home to a community of painters, artists of a realist school who took their canvases out of doors to paint real people in local settings. Artists such as Stanhope Forbes, Harold and Laura Knight and Frank Bramley were among the founders of what became known as the 'Newlyn School', and their paintings have left a valuable record of the lives of ordinary people.

By the beginning of the 20th century Newlyn was booming, as both a successful fishing port and a place famous for its artists. But as the century went on things didn't go so well for the chapel. As in other places of worship, in Cornwall and beyond, attendances fell and the church lost its role at the centre of the local community. Even so, the chapel continued to hold services until the end of the 20th century, when a threatened ceiling collapse forced the congregation to abandon it for the adjacent Sunday School and the local Seamen's Mission.

There have been other changes in Newlyn too. Although the fishing fleet is still successful, the market building needs upgrading and so do many of the boats. Meanwhile, Newlyn has become a popular holiday destination and many of its houses are now second homes. If plans to regenerate the area bring still further holiday accommodation, many locals will resist. Planners face the challenge of catering for visitors while also serving Newlyn's unique working community.

The chance to restore the chapel is a chance to give Newlyn back one of its most precious resources. The asbestos roof could be replaced with slate, and with heating installed the interior could be restored to incorporate exhibition space. This will require plenty of ingenuity, since the box pews make the interior difficult to convert. But, as Julyan Drew explains, 'With the advice of experts from English Heritage we are learning to think of ways of using the building creatively while also respecting its important fixtures and fittings. There is space behind the pulpit, for example, which could be used for display. And another idea is to replace the vestry with a glazed extension. The building has evolved in the past and the time has come for it to adapt a little more in order to survive into the future.'

Displays could tell the fascinating story of Newlyn's fishing and other industries, its people and its painters. As Julyan Drew puts it: 'Newlyn has lots of stories to tell, and lots of material to tell these stories. At the moment, for example, there is very little information on display about the Newlyn artists. The chapel could help fill this gap and by adapting the building in this way we could make it a creative force for the future.' Together with the Newlyn Gallery and Penlee Museum, among other sites, the chapel could become both a visitor attraction and a special and beautiful focus of justifiable local pride. ■

Dawe's Twine Works

Trinity Chapel

Welcombe Barton

South East

The South East seems to have the best of both worlds. Stretching from Kent and Essex in the east to Hampshire in the west, it has a large population, with two major city areas – the Medway towns and Brighton and Hove, each with a population of around 250,000 – as well as dozens of smaller towns and the vast urban magnet of London. Many of its towns are both handsome and prosperous. The South East is, by most available measures, the richest part of the United Kingdom, an area full of corporate headquarters, successful young high-tech industries and prestigious research establishments. Good transport links to the rest of the country and to Europe complete the picture.

To go with the material advantages there are also natural riches. This is a region with a remarkable environment. Some 6,500 square kilometres in the South East are designated as areas of outstanding natural beauty (AONBs). The South East's AONBs range from the New Forest to the South Downs and their acreage makes up one third of the country's total AONB land. There are also further stretches of land that are earmarked as Green Belt, Sites of Special Scientific Interest, or some other designation.

The natural conditions have had a huge influence on the region's traditional building styles. In the heart of the area, across large swathes of Surrey, Sussex and Kent, lies the Weald, an area that is clay underfoot and was

MASSEY'S FOLLY
Upper Farringdon, Hampshire

WATTS GALLERY
Compton, Surrey

once largely covered with trees. Around the Wealden clay lie bands of stone, including chalk, greensand and other rocks, providing the region with a variety of building stone. Nevertheless, in past centuries the most widespread styles of traditional architecture featured wood, in the form of timber frames and weatherboarding, and clay, in the form of locally made bricks and tiles.

The villages of the South East still boast many timber-built houses. Some have wooden frames infilled with brick or pale wattle and daub. Others are clad with horizontal weatherboarding. Many farms in the South East have weatherboarded barns, blackened with tar or creosote to keep out the water. Some towns and villages also have streets of weatherboarded houses, their wooden cladding either black or painted bright white. Many of these houses have been re-clad sometime during their history, and from the 18th century onwards it was increasingly likely that the new cladding would be imported pine. Paint, tar or some other form of waterproofing is vital to preserve such material, but with proper care it can last for hundreds of years.

The combination of rich clay deposits with plenty of wood for fuel produced a thriving industry of brick- and tile-making in the South East. Red clay tiles were the prevalent roofing material throughout much of the region for centuries, and villages still boast many houses with tiled roofs, frequently covered with colonies of lichens that lend a palette of browns, yellows and oranges to the warm red of the clay. The tiles often go down the walls too, for they were an attractive and long-lasting alternative to weatherboarding.

Timber, tile and glowing red brick are just three of the materials that give the villages of the South East their warm variety. But as in most areas of Britain, the further you look the more variety you will find, with areas of chalk and flint, houses faced with beach pebbles, and a range of pinkish, greenish and greyish stones appearing in various localities across the region. Set these buildings against an equally rich landscape backdrop ranging from pasture to hop farms, downland to valley bottoms, and the South East has a rural environment second to none.

This region, then, seems to have everything going for it, but this is not the whole story. For one thing, this rich area contains pockets of poverty that are all too easy to miss and some of the region's towns, notably Hastings, Southampton and Medway, score high in the government's indices of deprivation.

And even the most prosperous towns and villages have their problems. Partly this is because of their very success. A buoyant economy, especially when combined with a pleasant environment, attracts new residents by the thousand, increasing demand for property and forcing up house prices. In AONBs and other

designated areas, planning restrictions make it more difficult to build new houses so prices are pushed up again. There soon comes a point when low-paid people can only afford to live in the poorer towns which are often far away from where they work. This process tends to ghettoise entire areas as either rich or poor and also adds to the traffic, with more and more people having to travel further to their place of work.

Changes like this can have a huge effect on villages. Once even smaller villages were holistic communities; they included people of a wide range of income levels, age groups and professions, and they had the kind of vibrant life that could sustain all sorts of facilities, from shops to schools. But house-price rises have squeezed the poor and the young out of many villages in the richer parts of the South East and some of the facilities that they used have vanished too, making it more difficult to attract them back.

The disappearance of many traditional rural jobs has contributed to these trends. New jobs have come to replace them but they have often brought new workers too, and the region's close proximity to London has made its villages attractive to commuters. So some south-eastern villages slumber during weekdays, only coming to life at the weekends and in the evenings when the workers pour off the trains from the city.

But the region has been influenced by London for hundreds of years — it is inevitable, given the capital's proximity. And the situation does have its positive side: Londoners and those with connections to the capital can give much to the region, and do. All three south-eastern restoration candidates in their different ways demonstrate the benefit of these ties between country and city. A building like Massey's Folly in Upper Farringdon, for example, could not have been built without its creator's knowledge of the wider world of architecture. It is an architectural fish out of water perhaps, but this is what gives it its charm. The Woodrolfe Granary at Tollesbury is very much a local building, but it is also a very special reminder both of coastal trade and of the links between country and city that were fostered by the yachting craze of the early 20th century. The Watts Gallery celebrates in a totally different way the traffic between the capital and the countryside. It was the work of two London artists who came to the country for health reasons and brought immeasurable benefits to their adopted community.

So the three candidates, for all their variety, show how the South East could take advantage of the challenges of London while producing buildings that serve their villages too. Restoration of the buildings would multiply these advantages, renewing the local benefits while attracting visitors who will enjoy and understand the region all the more for learning about its fascinating history. ■

Woodrolfe Granary
Tollesbury, Essex

"The granary was the centre of life around the estuary and a meeting point for everyone – chandlers and fitters, fishermen and labourers, yacht-owners and skippers."

For most of its history Tollesbury has been shaped by the sea. The place stands on a small rise overlooking the Blackwater estuary and from here people have been watching boats coming and going for centuries. Fishing vessels, cargo craft, racing yachts and pleasure boats – all have been important to this Essex community.

It is still a thriving, busy place, as Julian Goldie, Managing Partner of the Woodrolfe Boatyard, comments: 'Although some people from the village commute to Colchester and beyond, there is a vibrant light-industrial estate that provides employment for local people. In addition the marina brings in a lot of visitors and generates tourist income for Tollesbury – many people from the boats go to the village to eat, drink and buy provisions. Some also walk along the sea wall to look at the coastal scenery and wildlife habitats.' The Woodrolfe Granary, not far from the modern yacht harbour, is close to the centre of all this activity.

As far back as the Bronze Age people were producing salt on the nearby marshes, while in the Iron Age and Roman times the estuary was a stopping-off point for boats trading with Europe. But it was after the Romans left, when the Saxons began to set up their kingdoms in the 5th century, that the place got its identity. Tollesbury is a Saxon name – it was probably the burh, or fortified settlement, of a Saxon called Tol in the kingdom of the East Saxons, or Essex as we call it today.

From Saxon times to the 17th century the place was owned by a succession of noble families and churchmen, all of whom no doubt valued its strategic site near the river. But it was in the 19th century, when Tollesbury was firmly in the hands of the trading middle classes, that it became really

prosperous. The census of 1851 reveals a host of different businesses – blacksmiths, bricklayers, carriers, millers, saddlers, sea wallers, thatchers, a watchmaker and a wheelwright. There were fishermen and others who made their living from the sea. And last but not least there were numerous farmers and 145 farm workers, the bosses no doubt benefiting from the excellent transport links that could take their produce to a range of different markets.

This is where the granary comes in, as a storage depot for grain and other produce that was transported up and down the estuary and along the Essex coast. In fact it is likely that the other products took precedence, since there is some doubt about whether the building's wooden structure would have been strong enough for a heavy load of grain.

Today this structure appears flimsy. It is a timber-framed building covered with wooden

Opposite The granary stands right by the waterside, a position that was ideal when it came to loading and unloading cargoes but which has also made the building vulnerable to water at high tides.

Above Inside, the building's plight is clear. Many of the structural timbers are sound but there are floorboards and wall cladding missing everywhere.

Clockwise from top left Substantial joists show that this was a solid, well-built structure; broad doors gave access to big loads; the props that originally supported the building are eroding away; steep stairs lead to the upper level.

Opposite A view of an end wall shows how the building was modified to provide more room upstairs.

weatherboarding and provided with big doors and long rows of windows. A roof of corrugated iron keeps out the rain. A lot of the timber cladding is broken or missing and there are gaps between the floorboards, but much of the framework that holds it all together is solid. It has also survived alteration over the years. To begin with the granary was a structure of one-and-a-half storeys; in other words there were two floors, the upper one in the roof space beneath a tile-covered, half-hipped roof. Today, however, the building has a taller, more spacious upper floor.

Its site by the water meant the building was always in the middle of the bustle of docking barges and fishing boats. Fishing had been a major local activity for centuries and the fishermen were always ready to adapt to demands for different kinds of catch. When the granary was built the oyster trade was the biggest money-spinner. The 1851 census recorded 112 people

employed in the oyster trade, and the number increased steadily over the next few decades. But towards the end of the century the demand for oysters declined and Tollesbury's boats went out in search of sprat, herring and shrimp. There was also a thriving business 'five-fingering', or collecting starfish for fertiliser, before this trade was killed by alternative fertilisers in the 1920s. But the shrimping and herring fishing continued.

So did the cargo-carrying business. A speciality of the area was broad-beamed 'stackie' barges, so wide they could carry a haystack and shallow enough to navigate up small creeks. When a stack had been loaded the high cargo meant the skipper could not see which way to steer; his mate had to get up on top of the stack and shout instructions down, a job that required split-second timing and perfect understanding between skipper and mate. This was not for everyone and the Blackwater also had more

conventional barges, known locally as 'boomies', which carried other cargoes. Their loads included coal from Newcastle, ragstone from Kent, new potatoes from Jersey, flint for road-making, and timber from various sources. All were handled by Tollesbury boats and their skippers had to adapt their skills to suit the goods they were carrying and the customers they worked for.

In the 1920s the granary too was adapted. The walls were raised, more windows were added, and the half-hipped roof was replaced by a gabled arrangement. This provided more height and light in the upper storey, but the attractive tiles were replaced by corrugated iron – a cheap and serviceable material for a working building. The alterations to the building signalled bigger changes. By the 1920s the barge trade was in decline and road transport was on the increase; it was faster, less labour-intensive and less dependent on the weather. Fewer and fewer barges put in at Tollesbury and the need for produce-storage facilities disappeared.

But there was already a new business taking over. Since the mid-19th century the area had been associated with competitive yachting. Several of the America's Cup yachts had been built at Tollesbury and some of the fishermen, who had got a taste for speed when they raced their boats home after a night at sea, became competitive skippers.

This new trend meant a big change for Tollesbury. Instead of fishermen and cargo-carriers the place became the haunt of well-heeled late Victorian and Edwardian boat owners, people who could spend a fortune on a pleasure yacht or a racing craft. The old granary was already close to the centre of this new business when, in the 1920s, it took on a major role in Tollesbury's expanding boat-building industry.

The roomy granary was used for a while for boat-building and repairing nets, but its main role was as an office for the boat-builders. This meant that it became a general meeting place and social centre for everyone locally involved in the trade. It became the place to meet friends and colleagues, enjoy a tea break and swap gossip and stories. People even took to coming to the old granary on Sundays because it was a centre where hands, craftsmen and rich yacht-owners could meet and talk. The granary was the busy heart of the boatyard and harbour,

Village Voice

"The granary is the first thing that the fishermen and yachtsmen saw as they came up to Tollesbury, and it's still an important part of Tollesbury life. But it's not just for Tollesbury people. When people come to the village, they look at the marshes and wonder what the history is, and we're hoping that they'll be able to find out in the granary."

FAY HEARD Tollesbury

and many people still remember it with affection.

It was a good time for Tollesbury. Money came into the area and the boatmen were ready to earn their share. Many did well sailing in racing yachts and some moved into smart modern houses on Woodrolfe Road. But by the end of the 1920s Britain's period of success in yacht racing was over, and by the middle of the 20th century the area's yachting economy had declined sharply.

For the granary, there was another problem. Periodical flooding had allowed the brackish water of the estuary to eat away at the wooden piles that held up the structure. Gradually some of these were replaced with more solid masonry supports, but rises in sea level made flooding a constant threat that promised to wash the building away if nothing was done to protect it.

So Tollesbury's much-loved old granary began to slide into decline. Pleasure craft have come back to the Blackwater, there is a smart 1960s yacht harbour and some of the riverside buildings have been restored, but the battered old granary has not been so lucky. Further rises in the sea level that are likely to come with climate change make its fate more precarious as the years go by.

But now there is hope: there are plans to lift the framework a further half-metre off the ground. Julian Goldie explains: 'Raising the granary will take it out of danger from the high spring tides that wash through the building at the moment. Once it has been raised it will only flood twice a year, at the equinoctial tides. And a novel display system, suspended from the ceiling, has been devised to keep displays off the floor and clear of the flood waters when they do come.' Once the building has been raised there can be a thorough restoration, keeping as much as possible of the original timber framework and boarding but renewing this where necessary. The interior can then be fitted out .

Upstairs, exhibition space is planned. The building could play host to school parties during the week and environmental groups at weekends. All could look out on the area's salt marshes, as well as learning from the displays and objects exhibited. Downstairs a meeting room for local people and groups, plus further exhibition space, is planned. Lifts for disabled access are also part of the scheme. Those who remember the building's heyday before the boatyard was closed in the 1950s recall that the granary was the centre of life around the estuary and a meeting point for everyone – chandlers and fitters, fishermen and labourers, yacht-owners and skippers. They look forward to the time when it can be a vibrant gathering-place once more. ∎

Opposite Battered by waves and scoured by salt, the timbers of the granary still have a beauty all their own.

Below A view from the granary showing some of the boats that still make Tollesbury a hive of activity.

Massey's Folly
Upper Farringdon, Hampshire

Right The red-brick folly stands out against the prevailing local backdrop of white cottages and greenery.

Opposite Massey went for diversity in everything: heights, gable shapes, window sizes — all are triumphantly varied.

We all have a picture in our minds of the ideal village. Its appearance would vary from place to place but the overriding impression would be one of harmony – small cottages and farms mostly built in local materials, leafy gardens, a church spire poking up in the background. We don't expect too many surprises. But occasionally a village can pull off a really big surprise, and there is none bigger or more dramatic than Massey's Folly in the Hampshire village of Upper Farringdon.

In this area of white-walled thatched cottages and green fields, the building that dominates Upper Farringdon is a red-brick alien, a vast structure clad in stunning terracotta panels and topped by ornate towers. Local resident Donna Corbin sums up the usual reaction of the many tourists who come to Upper Farringdon: 'Everyone who comes to the village asks what Massey's Folly is and why it is here. At first they are amazed by the building's sheer incongruity – they can't believe that anyone would put up a structure like this in a village full of thatched cottages. But when they look again they see the Folly's extraordinary beauty.'

So how *did* it come to be built? The answer to this question only leads to further mysteries. Massey's Folly was built by the Rev Thomas Hackett Massey, who was rector of Upper Farringdon from 1857 until he died in 1919. In 1870 Massey bought a building in the village called the Stone House, demolished it, and began to build afresh. Work went slowly because

> "The hall was used for wedding receptions, parties, dances and Parish Council meetings. In the 1940s and 1950s, before widespread car ownership, the place thrived."

Massey used only three workers – a bricklayer, a labourer and a carpenter – and designed the building himself as he went along. When bricklayer Henry Andrews produced a stretch of wall that Massey was not happy with it was demolished and Andrews had to begin again.

This whole process took about 40 years and what emerged was a building with some 17 bedrooms, a hall, a number of sitting rooms and a pair of towers. At one end a huge semicircular gable pops up, clad in patterns of terracotta. All over the walls there are terracotta tiles moulded with fruit, leaves, fleur-de-lys symbols and flowers. The architectural style is a mishmash, with parts influenced by French and Spanish buildings of the Middle Ages and parts apparently dreamed up by Massey himself. Some people have even seen an Indian influence in the design. But this is a Victorian building and the Victorians were uninhibited in their invention, always delighting in borrowing and adapting different architectural styles from all over the world. And for all its variety the building is of a piece – the overall use of red brick and ornate terracotta panels that glow with colour in the sunlight gives the building a character and unity all its own.

In 1910 Henry Andrews laid down his trowel and Massey declared the building complete. But instead of opening it, he boarded it up. What was going on? What was the building meant to be for

and why was it not being used? Massey was very secretive about his purposes and does not seem to have told his parishioners what he was building. Interviewed by the *Morning Leader* newspaper in 1906, he said rather hesitantly, 'I believe I shall make a tea-house out of it.' Tea-rooms and tea-houses, where independent women could go for a meal or snack without entering the male-dominated world of the pub, were all the rage in Edwardian England. But Massey did not seem committed to the catering business. Was there another answer to the mystery?

The *Morning Leader* seemed to think so. Obviously unconvinced by Massey's reply, the *Leader*'s reporter put forward some more theories: was it to be a lunatic asylum, or a fruitarian hospital – an institution caring for the sick and feeding them fruit, vegetables and dairy produce, one of the fashionable diets of the time? The rector could have been evasive because he wanted to avoid local objections to the arrival of large numbers of people, possibly the mentally ill, in their village.

There was even gossip that the building was a kind of Victorian Taj Mahal, a tribute to a woman from India whom Massey admired: Emily Parker, the illegitimate daughter of an Englishman who worked in the Indian Civil Service. She lived in Upper Farringdon from the late 19th century and Massey provided her with a cottage. Some people said that she helped the rector with the design of

Village Voice

"If we attend to the function of the building as well as the fabric and make it a full community resource, then I think people will love it in different ways."

NIGEL PINK Upper Farringdon

his building and that its vaguely Indian appearance was due to her influence. But Massey was as secretive about his relationship with Emily as about the purpose of his folly, and the story is only a rumour.

A more likely explanation involves Massey's religious views. Massey was a high churchman, a follower of a movement in the Victorian Anglican church to restore some of the church's earlier heritage. The leaders of this movement included powerful churchmen such as John Henry Newman, John Keble and Edward Pusey. These were men who believed that the church was being increasingly dominated by the state, and argued for the church's autonomy and its spiritual power. They also set a high value on elaborate ritual and encouraged the building of beautifully decorated Gothic churches as fitting settings for their worship. They put forward their views in pamphlets known as tracts and became known as the Tractarians as a result.

Massey seems to have been a follower of the high-church ideas of the Tractarians. He disliked low churchmen and nonconformists such as Methodists, whose worship was still plainer and 'lower'. He even had a reputation for buying up property with Methodist connections and boarding it up, and the site of the folly itself had a history of Methodist links. Soon after arriving in Farringdon Massey rebuilt the chancel of his church in typical Tractarian style, giving it an ornate ceiling, rich tiling and marble altar furnishings from Florence that all contributed to the effect. He also removed the building's old box pews – another symbol of low-church history.

One of the trends connected with the high church and Tractarian movements was the revival of religious communities, especially communities of nuns. The English monasteries had been swept away in the 1530s under Henry VIII, but the Tractarians revived them and these Anglican communities were admired for their caring work with the poor and the sick. It may be that Massey was planning to form such a religious community in Upper Farringdon.

This is far from certain but it is a plausible theory, accounting for the bedrooms in the building and also for some of the symbolism used in the decoration. A prominent motif is the pomegranate, a fruit which in art is used to represent both the Christian church – with its many seeds standing for the church's many members – and, with its pink flesh, the suffering body of Christ. It seems likely that there was a strong religious motive behind Massey's obsessive building.

But Massey's plan, whatever it was, was never realised. Massey never lost faith in the building process but he lost touch with the village of Upper Farringdon. The villagers did not like the changes he brought in the church or his curious, secretive habits, and they were probably

Above left Panels of flower and fruit decoration are framed by repeated terracotta blocks of nail-head (the tiny raised pyramids) and simplified flowers.

Above right Massey's bricklayer devised these corbelled courses of brickwork to manage the meeting of levels at this awkward corner.

Opposite Even from the side the eccentricity is maintained, with blind openings combining with the repertoire of terracotta ornament.

suspicious of what might happen in his big red building too. The village boys delighted in pushing him into ditches – though in typical eccentric fashion Massey seemed to enjoy this and treated it as a game. The adults voted with their feet and trudged to the nearby parish of Chawton for their Sunday service. On most Sundays only the faithful Henry Andrews and Massey's laundry-woman attended his church.

Massey died lonely, and probably unfulfilled, in 1919. But his wonderful folly remained. The executors of Massey's will decided that it would make a good school and village hall and the people of Upper Farringdon responded enthusiastically, no doubt relieved that the folly was not to become a haven for psychiatric patients or fruitarians. They acted quickly to raise the money needed to refit the building and were soon holding fêtes, concerts, whist drives and jumble sales to raise the £1,800 needed. By 1925 the folly had become a new school and a public hall that local groups could use. The Farringdon Men's Club (membership 3 old pence per week, intoxicating liquor forbidden) met there regularly, as did the Women's Institute. The hall was used for wedding receptions, parties, dances and Parish Council meetings. In the 1940s and 1950s, before widespread car ownership enabled people to travel further afield for their entertainment, the place thrived, and the school remained there until it closed in 1987.

The building is still much used today. Although the southern half was sold, the northern portion is still the scene of meetings, a thriving nursery and evening classes. But the old building is now seriously dilapidated and the problems are more than a small community can solve on their own. As Donna Corbin explains: 'Some of the problems are due to the building's eccentric design. The complex roof has a number of valleys that are blocked or damaged and are letting in rainwater. And so paint is flaking off many of the walls and some of the ceilings are coming down. Large parts of the building are no longer fit for use.'

In 2005 the owner of the southern half was given permission to convert it into flats, but this decision was overturned to give the local people the chance to reunite the two halves of the building, restore the fabric and upgrade the facilities to give Upper Farringdon a superb community building.

It is a challenge, and a big project for a village of around 600 people. But plans have already been drawn up providing for a hall, shop, kitchen, café, terrace, various public rooms and two small flats. The flats could be let as holiday accommodation and the shop and café could also generate some of the income that will be needed to maintain the building in the future.

The organisers are undaunted by the size of the task. They are inspired by the fact that their small community has ownership of a unique but little known architectural gem which can become an enormous asset. And they can give the building the purpose it lacked in Massey's time. The Victorian rector's gesture of eccentricity could have an assured future and a permanent function at last. ▪

Above This room has become a repository for forgotten furniture. The damage to the wall finishes is clearly visible.

Below Massey's initials are picked out in terracotta. Whatever else the building was intended to be, it is a memorial to its creator.

Opposite The tower's brickwork glows in the sunlight.

Watts Gallery

Compton, Surrey

"The villagers dug the clay in the grounds of the Watts's house, carted it to the billiard room, and developed their modelling skills to produce the miles of ornament that were needed."

Above A statue of G F Watts, presiding genius of the gallery.

The painter George Frederic Watts was one of the great Victorians. Born in 1817, he established himself as an artist in 1843 when he was one of the winners of the competition for painters to produce works for the new Houses of Parliament. He made a deep study of the painters of the past, especially Venetian masters such as Titian and the greatest Renaissance artists, particularly Michelangelo.

Watts had a double career. He was one of the most successful portrait painters of his time, producing hundreds of likenesses of the most famous and prominent people of the era. But he did not think of the portraits as his most important work: Watts was more interested in producing paintings with some sort of moral message. Perdita Hunt, director of the Watts Gallery, explains: 'Watts believed that art was for all people. He saw his work as a form of communication, and he used his art to comment on the social issues of the time, such as the poverty suffered by working people, the distress caused by the Irish famine of the 1840s and the fate of women who committed suicide rather than endure the shame of giving birth to an illegitimate child.' He also painted allegorical paintings with titles like *Love Triumphant* and *Hope*, which were among the most popular paintings of the 19th century. Both these and the images of distressed workers appealed to the Victorian idea that art should have a moral purpose and should inspire people to live better lives.

So Watts's work had wide appeal, both to the wealthy men and women whose portraits he painted and to the middle-class art-lovers who displayed reproductions of his moral paintings in their homes. He was friends with most of the well-known artists and writers of the time, from Lewis Carroll and Alfred, Lord Tennyson, to fellow artists such as Edward Burne-Jones. He even fell in love with the most famous actress of the time, Ellen Terry, and the couple married in 1864. But the marriage did not last and Watts did not find happiness until he was 69, when he married the 36-year-old potter and amateur painter Mary Seton Fraser Tytler.

The couple had friends who lived at Compton, near Guildford, and they liked to visit them and stay in the area during the winter. In 1890 they decided to build their own house there. They

called the house Limnerslease, from two old words, for 'painter' and 'to glean'. Mary said she hoped, 'that there were golden years to be gleaned in this new home'. Little did she know how strong their links with Compton would become.

By the end of the 19th century G F Watts was so famous, and so rich, that he did not need to sell many of his paintings, so he began to stockpile his work and plan a gallery where it could be displayed. And so began the idea of the Watts Gallery, the first English gallery designed to exhibit the work of a single artist.

George and Mary Watts were enthusiasts of the Arts and Crafts movement, the school of

architects and designers who followed the teachings of the great Victorian writer and designer William Morris. From the 1870s onwards Arts and Crafts designers, who included architects such as Philip Webb and C F A Voysey, had developed a style of asymmetrical buildings with low, sweeping rooflines, often with walls covered with render. This was the style adopted by Christopher Hatton Turnor, the little-known Arts and Crafts architect commissioned by the Watts to design their gallery.

Turnor came up with a low-slung building with rendered walls and lots of gables, arranged around a central courtyard. In many ways it was a

Above The top-lit main gallery has always been richly decorated with bright paintwork and rugs.

Village Voice

"It was built right in the centre of Compton and it's still used and loved by the people in the area, and that's its history and that's what people are fascinated by. It's not just to see Watts, here you get much more, you get the paintings, you get the atmosphere, you get the building, the history and the community as well. It's a place to inspire and fascinate. It's unique."

MARK BILLS Compton

typical Arts and Crafts design with many of the usual decorative touches – stylised leaves and flowers on the lead-faced doors, ceramic tiles and fine interior woodwork. Today it blends beautifully into its rural surroundings but this countrified look was only part of the story. The interior was vibrant with colour, with a paint scheme of 'green apple', grey and gold, and Persian carpets on the floors.

The gallery has an intriguing structural secret. Beneath the pale rendering the walls of this traditional-looking building are made of the most modern material: concrete. Apparently Turnor had visited America where he got to know the inventor Thomas Edison, who was trying to promote the use of concrete to build low-cost houses. Turnor caught the concrete bug too and used the material in the construction of the Watts gallery in the early 1900s, 20 years before modernist architects began to adopt it seriously in their buildings. Perdita Hunt emphasises the building's liveliness and modernity: 'When it was built it represented cutting-edge design. The finishes were bright, the architect had used new materials, the canvases glowed in the changing natural light. And the place was full of life. After all, it is a gallery, not a museum.'

Turnor's use of concrete shows his practicality too. Some Arts and Crafts architects insisted on traditional materials and hand-made craftsmanship throughout but Turnor was prepared to explore a different way of building. Other innovative touches came from the special demands of the complex and its users. There are bedrooms for Mary Watts's apprentices and a special corridor to allow them to move around without going through the gallery itself. A tall, narrow door allows Watts's large canvases to be moved in and out and there is even an under-floor heating system, though this was less of an innovation than it seems: the architect bought it second-hand, another example of his pragmatic approach.

The gallery was built in 1903 and the following year the artist's vast collection of his own paintings was quickly hung. The gallery opened in 1904 (shortly before Watts's death on 1 July). It was a huge achievement, and the large collection of work by this popular artist drew great interest.

But the collection was so large that it was hard to display it all properly. Soon Mary had an extension built, in more conventional brick. She

added what is now the main gallery together with a space to display her husband's sculptures, bringing the doors from his old studio in Kensington. These additions were ready by 1906, by which time the place was already full of people learning the potter's craft from Mary, who had begun holding classes at Limnerslease in 1895.

Mary was just as much of a visionary as her husband. But while G F Watts aimed to teach morality by painting inspiring subjects, Mary wanted to lead people to fulfilment through teaching her skills as a potter. And she knew there was a need – country life around Compton in the 1890s was bitterly hard. Agriculture was in depression and at the best of times farm work was punishingly tough.

Mary wanted to lift people out of poverty by giving them marketable skills. And so she began to teach clay modelling and pottery at Limnerslease, soon extending this by building a proper pottery and taking in more pupils from the surrounding area. At one point she was teaching up to 70 people from in and around Compton, and another 14 to 18 apprentices from farther afield lived on site. Like her husband and the rest of their artistic circle, they were inspired by the ideas of Arts and Crafts luminaries such as William Morris and John Ruskin, who insisted that traditional, skilled craft-work brought more satisfaction than toil in a factory. And they must have been right, because Mary's classes

continued to be extremely popular.

Soon after the classes began Mary and her apprentices took on another project, a chapel that was built as a monument to her husband and was a showcase for the art of decorative ceramics. Bands of terracotta ornament and figures of angels run around the chapel's curving outside walls, in a style that combines motifs from Italy with the kind of decoration found on old Celtic manuscripts.

The villagers seem to have taken to the task of creating the chapel with enthusiasm. They dug the clay in the grounds of the Watts's house, carted it to the billiard room, which had been turned into a workshop, and developed their modelling skills to produce the miles of ornament that were needed. Sometimes as many as 40 students turned up to the class and people of all ages, from 10 to 60, responded keenly to Mary's teaching. The finished chapel is extraordinary and is an amazing celebration of the craftsmanship of Mary Watts and her village pupils.

The interior of the chapel, which Mary completed in 1906 after her husband's death, is in a different style, the then-fashionable Art Nouveau. Ranks of angels are surrounded by swathes of curving lines in a dark palette of gold, reds and greens. There is nothing quite like it anywhere in Britain.

Indeed there is nothing quite like this complex of gallery and chapel, a unique tribute to an artist

Above left The Watts Chapel, built for the village cemetery and as a memorial to the artist. *Above right* Decoration for the chapel was made in the studio by Mary Watts and her pupils.

Opposite A view of the pottery where Mary Watts worked and taught.

Opposite This door bears Watts's motto: 'The utmost for the Highest', summing up the artist's philosophy.

Left Richard Jefferies, curator, sits in his study at Compton.

Below, left to right Details at the gallery: a roundel set in one of the gables; grilles revealing the heating system; a wooden-framed window.

who caught the mood of the late 19th century. But the gallery is now more than 100 years old and is showing its age. Water has found its way in through the roof, there are cracks in the walls and the old under-floor heating system is failing. The gallery space also needs to be brought up to modern standards, with proper environmental controls, to preserve Watts's unique pictorial legacy. This proposed work would be part of a wider scheme, involving conserving the pictures, providing better storage, and upgrading visitor facilities, including making the gallery fully accessible to people with disabilities.

It is a big scheme and will require something like the determination that drove Mary Watts to extend the gallery and build the chapel. But it will be worth it – not just because Watts and his work are of national importance, but also because of the value it will bring to the local area. Mary Watts's vision was one of artists and villagers working together; in fact the villagers themselves became artists and craftspeople. The restoration of the Watts Gallery could put arts and crafts back at the heart of village life once more. ■

Woodrolfe Granary

Massey's Folly

ALL SAINTS' CHURCH
Beckingham, Lincolnshire

Midlands & East Anglia

This region covers the whole of the central area of England, taking in the mainly rural counties of Herefordshire and Shropshire in the west, the much more populous and urbanised areas around Birmingham, and the quieter East Midlands and East Anglia. It therefore comprises several regions in one, with all the diversity that this implies. The landscape ranges from the bare and moor-like uplands of Derbyshire, to Nottinghamshire's gently undulating fields, to the low-lying areas of fenland and farmland in Lincolnshire and East Anglia.

The villages of the Midlands are just as varied. As we travel across this vast swathe of middle England, the appearance of the typical village changes with the local building materials, as timber gives way to stone and stone yields to brick. In the far west, in counties such as Herefordshire and Worcestershire, the traditional building material was timber and there are still many 'black and white' villages of timber-framed houses surrounded by apple orchards and fields of hops or fruit. In the East Midlands, by contrast, there is a long tradition of stone building. Northamptonshire, for example, is in the heart of the belt of limestone that stretches across the country and its golden stone villages are justly famous. But the Midlands has other good building stone too – sandstones and marlstones for example – that give some of the buildings of Nottinghamshire and Leicestershire

PENNOYER'S SCHOOL
Pulham St Mary, Norfolk

CHEDHAM'S YARD
Wellesbourne, Warwickshire

Clockwise from right
A collection of stained-glass fragments makes a splash of colour in one of the windows at All Saints' Church; part of an old sign for a business in Warwick hangs at Chedham's Yard; initials are carved into the brickwork of Pennoyer's School.

All these features are examples of how the accidents of time can add interest and texture to a building.

their characteristic patina. And then there are the bricks and clay tiles, used widely for 300 years and common in many eastern areas, from Leicestershire to Lincolnshire.

People still think of the Midlands as an industrial area. It has a long history of all sorts of industry, from manufacturing in Birmingham to mining in Nottinghamshire, but much of the region is a rural landscape of fields and farms, and has been since the Middle Ages. As in any agricultural area, however, there was industry too, made up of small local businesses that existed to service the farms, their equipment and their machinery. But much of this industry, consisting of joiners and blacksmiths, stoneworkers and wheelwrights, declined with the onset of mass production. The increased mechanisation of farming, which required complex machinery and specialists to service it, struck a further blow to many of these old skills.

Farming has had to cope with as many setbacks here as in the rest of the country, and now the land is valued as much as a tourist attraction as an agricultural resource. Tourism employs hundreds of thousands of people in the Midlands and visitors come to learn about Shakespeare's birthplace, walk on the uplands of the Peak District, or travel by boat across the Norfolk Broads.

In spite of this, vast areas of the Midlands and eastern England remain little known by the majority of British people. In some cases this is because parts of the region are tucked away at the edges of England. Few people visit Herefordshire, for example, and Lincolnshire is one of the quietest and most isolated of all English counties, yet both are places of great rural beauty. Other areas are little known precisely because the transport links are so good – most visitors rush through them on the way to somewhere else. All many people know of Leicestershire is the M1, and for some the same is true of Staffordshire and the M6.

But the countryside is not just for tourists. Planners and countryside experts in the Midlands see the region facing several key challenges in the next few years. Among these are maintaining the quality of the area's green spaces; supporting rural businesses and helping them adapt to change while remaining rooted in the countryside; and fostering vibrant, active communities. It is clear that the villages of the Midlands and East Anglia have a vital role to play in all of this. Most are surrounded by fields, commons and other green spaces and village people are on the front line of looking after these vital resources. Villages are also home to rural industries and are places where we can learn about industries of the past, as Chedham's Yard in Warwickshire demonstrates. And above all they have the potential to be dynamic communities in which everyone plays an important role and for which historic buildings, sometimes adapting to change like everything else, have a key part to play.

These initiatives are aimed fairly and squarely at helping local people at home and at work. Nevertheless, tourism remains a major industry in the Midlands, and villages play an increasingly important part in this business. It is not simply that visitors require accommodation and like staying in picturesque country inns or traditional village cottages. Increasingly, people want to learn about the places they are visiting, and village buildings are crucial in this, not just as a backdrop but in the actual process of helping people discover the region's history. But village buildings are primarily there because they fulfilled local needs and, although these needs have changed, the buildings can still provide for them in different ways, as the region's three restoration candidates amply demonstrate.

The oldest of the three candidates is All Saints' Church, at Beckingham in Lincolnshire. Like thousands of other parish churches it is medieval, but it is an outstanding example of its type, with real potential to become again what it was for hundreds of years before: the heart and soul of its village. The building lay dormant for several years but the community has already started to bring it back to life, and can see the huge potential it will offer when completely restored. The same is true of Pennoyer's School in Pulham St Mary's, Norfolk, a unique building that combines a medieval guild chapel and a Victorian school and promises to provide its village with a much-needed gathering space. Chedham's Yard in Wellesbourne, Warwickshire, is testimony to an industry once-prevalent in the region but now largely vanished; it is a perfect example of a 'time-capsule' building, in which the contents tell endless stories about the craftspeople who used them.

Church, school and workshop sum up much of what was important in village life until the late 20th century when church-going declined, hundreds of village schools closed and rural industries were abandoned. The custodians of all these buildings have inspiring plans to make them once more vital to their villages. ▪

All Saints' Church
Beckingham, Lincolnshire

Opposite From the tall tower at one end to the low chancel at the other, All Saints' has been rebuilt several times over the centuries, but most of the details visible in this view are medieval.

Right It was quite common for churches to display a board with the names of those who had left money for the poor of the parish.

There is at least one place of worship in nearly every village and many of our churches are of enormous historical and architectural interest. The figures are extraordinary. There are more than 16,000 listed places of worship in Britain. The vast majority of these are Anglican parish churches and many of them – probably as many as 10,000 – were built before Henry VIII made the break with the Roman Catholic Church in the 1530s.

These medieval churches have a special character. The majority have changed and grown across the centuries, as the wealth of the parish has allowed and as religious and architectural fashions have changed, so it is not uncommon for a church to have been extended several times over the centuries. In many cases various restorations, especially in the Victorian period, will have left their mark on the building, and fixtures and fittings may date from many periods.

All Saints', Beckingham, is a good example of this kind of building, but it is a building at a point of crisis. Rev Dr Alan Megahey, rector of Beckingham, describes what it was like when he arrived in 2001: 'The building was in a dreadful state. It was closed for safety reasons, there were pigeon droppings everywhere, and the structure, especially the roofs, needed a lot of work.' It was a sad state of affairs for a church that had been looked after for 800 years.

All Saints' is the parish church of a village in western Lincolnshire, not far from Newark in nearby Nottinghamshire. Beckingham probably developed as a village in the Saxon and Norman periods – the centuries on either side of the Norman invasion of 1066. We know that there was a church here by the time the Normans carried out their Domesday survey in 1086 but

"In the late 18th century the vicar appealed for funds from parishioners, and his success was recorded on boards (now in the tower), which note each contributor and the amount they gave."

Above Graceful pointed arches of the 13th century separate the nave and aisles of All Saints' church.

Right Peeling plasterwork, evidence of damp, is one of the problems in the church's interior.

Opposite Rising above the churchyard trees, the church tower, with its tall pinnacles, is a landmark in the village.

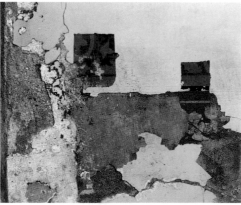

we cannot tell for sure whether any part of the present church is as old as that. The building certainly goes back at least to the 12th century when the two main doorways, both ornately carved in the Norman style, were built. The crisp carving around the doorways displays several Norman motifs, the most obvious being the zigzag and nail-head patterns – the latter like repeated, tiny raised pyramids. The stunning north doorway also displays carvings of little faces, animals and leaves. It is highly ornate work and in the 12th century there must have been a patron here, perhaps the lord of the manor, who could afford to employ a highly skilled mason.

For the next few centuries the people of Beckingham altered and extended their church as funds allowed. In the 13th century there was a major rebuilding, with the addition of side aisles – each separated from the central nave by a set of handsome pointed arches – the building of a south porch and the complete reconstruction of the chancel. All these changes probably had their origins in specific religious needs. The aisles, as well as providing more space for the congregation, would also have enabled the inclusion of more altars. The porch, as well as sheltering the main entrance, would also have been used for some religious ceremonies – marriages, for example, were conducted at the church door in the Middle Ages. And the revamping of the chancel, the part of the church used and maintained by the clergy, was a common occurrence in the 13th century, a period when ritual was becoming more elaborate and the number of items used in services, from books to sacred vessels, was multiplying.

In the 14th century the aisle walls were rebuilt and given larger windows. The walls above the nave arches were also raised and pierced with windows to let in more light from above. In the following century All Saints' substantial bell tower was added, with its bell chamber, large west window and tall pinnacles pointing heavenwards. All these alterations were done in the Gothic style, with pointed arches and ornate windows divided into sections with stone tracery, and by the end of the 15th century All Saints' had developed into the typical English Gothic parish church, with details from a number of rebuildings but an overall feeling of unity. Only the round-headed Norman north doorway (which must have been moved from its original position to be placed in the 13th- or 14th-century aisle wall) is in marked contrast to most of the rest of the church.

And so the church remained, though in at least one historical period its structure was seriously at risk. During the English Civil War of the 1640s nearby Newark was a royalist stronghold and was repeatedly besieged by the parliamentarians. The parliamentarian army camped at Beckingham for a while and, often short of money and resources, took what they could from the local area. One victim was the lead covering of the church roof, much of which was removed to make shot to fire at Newark.

As well as the repeated alterations, rebuildings and structural threats, All Saints', like most ancient churches, has also had more than one restoration during its long history. The first, so far as we know, took place in the late 18th century. The Archdeacon of Lincoln visited the church in 1786 and discovered that the building was in poor repair, 'particularly ye roof which is so ruinous as to be in some danger of falling'. The vicar appealed for funds from parishioners and his success was recorded on some boards

Village Voice

"Beckingham has lost its shop, it's lost its school, it's lost its post office. I think the post office was the last to go. We have a pub, an award-winning restaurant, and the church. If we can get the church back, not just as a centre of worship but as a centre of the community, and hopefully the wider community, we can get a bit more life going on in the village."

GILL GREEN Beckingham

(now in the tower), which note each contributor and the amount they gave.

Further work was done on the church in 1857–8, by the architect M C Bailey of Newark. This time, an important aspect of the job was adding extra seats. In the 1850s many parishioners paid rent on their pews – a useful way of raising money for the church but hard on the poorer members of the congregation. So a number of free seats were also provided and Bailey's restoration was an opportunity to include almost 30 more for the poor of the parish. There was a third restoration 30 years later, this time by Charles Hodgson Fowler, a Durham architect who specialised in church work. Fowler renewed the east windows and the roof of the chancel, and refaced some of the walls, notably the clerestory and the porch. Most of the church's fittings – such as the pews, screen and pulpit – are Victorian, designed by either Bailey or Fowler.

Many Victorian church restorations did a lot of damage. Victorian architects liked to tidy up the variations and what they saw as 'unevennesses' in medieval work, to give churches a more unified appearance. But All Saints' was fortunate. It escaped the worst excesses of the Victorian restorers and many of its medieval details were preserved though the chancel, with its renewed east windows, owes a lot to Fowler.

Little work was done on the building after the Victorian period and by the late 20th century there was a long list of required repairs. Now, however, with a new incumbent in place, there is new hope for the parish church of Beckingham. The first stage of the works, the reroofing of the chancel to make it once more fit for worship, is already complete. The next stage will be repairs to the nave and north aisle roofs. There is also the potential to restore some of the brightly coloured Victorian wall and ceiling decoration in the chancel. And there is a final stage: to turn All Saints' into a more versatile resource for the community. This entails installing better lighting and heating, removing some of the pews and fitting new flooring, and interior redecoration. A number of other facilities are planned, including a kitchen and internet café in the tower, and there is the possibility of installing a cash machine to provide another facility sorely lacking in the village. These are practical measures but the church is, above all, inspiring as a place of worship. As Alan Megahey

says: 'It looks good lit with candles for the carol service – the medieval nave and tower soar and the chancel, decorated with coloured Victorian tiles, glows richly.'

The proposed changes could make a huge difference to the village. Today Beckingham has no post office or shop and its village hall is so small it can only legally accommodate 60 people. But though there is no school, younger families are beginning to move to the village again, no doubt attracted by its convenient location near such major centres as Newark, and because it remains quiet despite being close to a major road. The church could once again become the centre of the community it was in the Middle Ages, a genuine resource for the whole village. ■

Top The stonework of the south porch at All Saints'.

Above Some of the old gravestones around the church have been moved from their original positions.

Opposite, clockwise from top left The south doorway; one of the 13th-century nave piers; one of the early clocks in the tower; a detail of the north doorway .

Pennoyer's School
Pulham St Mary, Norfolk

For much of the last century nearly every village of any size in Britain had its own school. Shrinking rural populations combined with widespread car ownership have meant that many of these small schools have been forced to close, usually to the sadness of local people who see the school as the heart of the village and a symbol of its future. Many of these schools were Victorian buildings, put up when education for all became a reality in the late 19th century. Some were older than this, tracing their beginnings back to charitable donations by local bigwigs of the 1600s or even earlier. Occasionally an early school like this can prove to be an architectural and historical treasure-trove, and this is the case with Pennoyer's School in the Norfolk village of Pulham St Mary.

At first glance Pennoyer's School looks like thousands of other small Victorian schools, with brick walls and tall classroom windows. But around the back is its secret: a chapel that dates to around 1401, before there was a school here at all. It is a guild chapel and, since guild chapels were usually incorporated into parish churches, it is a very rare building indeed.

The guilds were some of the most powerful institutions in the Middle Ages. They were basically trade associations, clubs formed by the members of a specific business or profession for mutual interest and support, but they also had a religious function. In medieval times, when everyone in Europe believed in the Christian God, people had a continuous preoccupation with the after-life. They believed that after death the soul would have to spend time in Purgatory before going to Heaven, and that time in Purgatory could be reduced by prayers and masses said after a person's death. The richest people built chantries and employed a priest to celebrate mass every day for their souls. Those who could not afford a chantry could attain the same goal through their guild, having a priest say mass for all its members. This is why guild chapels were so important.

In the Middle Ages one of the most important businesses in the Pulham area was hat- and cap-making, and at some point the hatters of Pulham formed a guild and had their chapel in the parish church. But in 1401 they decided to build a separate chapel, as the bishop's register at Ely records: '1401: Also on the 24th day of the said month of June, my Lord granted to all helping towards the re-establishment of the chapel of St James, within the parish of St Mary of Pulham, diocese of Norwich, and towards the support of Walter Colman the poor hermit there....'

Opposite The old chapel, with its walls of flint and its stone corner-buttresses, is attached at one end to the later school building. There is a low brick extension at the other end.

> "Pennoyer's School looks like thousands of other small Victorian schools. But around the back is its secret: a chapel that dates to around 1401."

Above The building has doors made of vertical planks of wood in the country style. A simple catch, with a metal handle to push and a thumb plate that lifts the latch inside, is the traditional way to secure such doors.

Below right Pulham St Mary was the base for vast airships in the early 20th century, a fact commemorated by the village sign, with its airship in low relief.

No one knows why the hatters of Pulham decided to move their chapel away from the parish church and create an independent building. It may be that they intended to set up a separate guild headquarters, with chapel and guildhall combined, although there is now no trace of a guildhall. Perhaps an increase in funds encouraged them to go it alone – or maybe they simply had a disagreement with the parish priest.

For whatever reason, by the beginning of the 15th century the hatters of Pulham had their own separate chapel and their own hermit to say prayers for them there. The prayers continued to be said by Walter Colman and his successors until the trade guilds were abolished in 1547, and the chapel itself remained virtually unchanged. The local manorial courts were held there for the next century or so, and a school was also started in the building, causing it to be preserved long after its original purpose had ceased.

Then in the 17th century a rich Puritan wool merchant, William Pennoyer, entered the history of Pulham St Mary. Pennoyer had bought a share in the manor and did well in business. He was a benefactor of Christ's Hospital School (then in London), founded various charities and even endowed Cambridge College in Massachusetts (now famous as Harvard University). On his death in 1670 he left various sums for charitable purposes, including funds to pay the teacher at the school in the old guild chapel.

Pennoyer's School carried on in the guild chapel into the Victorian period, which saw a huge expansion in education as state funding was provided to ensure education for all children. For the first time there was some expectation about the standards of school buildings, and many old schools also had to be extended because of the rising number of pupils. The guild chapel at Pulham was no longer deemed adequate for the local school and the building was extended and a typical red-brick Victorian school building was added. Its classrooms continued to serve the village children until, in 1988, it went the way of so many other rural primary schools and closed.

The people of Pulham St Mary are deeply attached to the school. Graham King, trustee of

Village Voice

"The number of times I've driven past and thought of all the happiness, all the work, all the industry that went on here, the memories that the children must have of the building."

MRS BLACK Pennoyer's School

the charity that is now responsible for the building, explains: 'Local people would be devastated if this building were closed for good. The school was paid for by the village, by the ancestors of some of those who live here today. Many locals attended the school as children. They don't want it to be sold to a private developer.' And they know they have something unique; because the Victorians kept the old chapel as part of their school, when the building closed it was the oldest state-school building in the country.

Historically speaking the medieval chapel is the most remarkable part of the building. It survives virtually complete except for the eastern wall where it joins the Victorian extension. The chapel is built mainly of flint, a typical building material in Norfolk where flints have been mined since the Stone Age. At Pulham the material gives the walls a pleasant brown and grey colouring which is more subtle than the Victorian brick that adjoins it. There is some decoration in the

Above A glazed partition in the Victorian school allows natural light to penetrate deeper into the building.

Left The classrooms in the Victorian school are both tall and light.

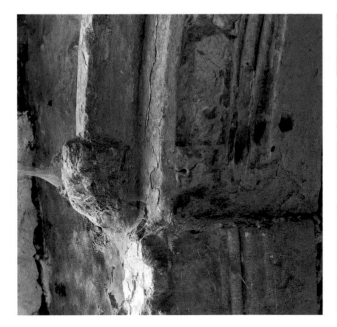

stonework, including delightful carved lions' heads that terminate the mouldings around the heads of several of the windows. There are also carved roses decorating the doorway, similar to ones on the fine porch of Pulham St Mary's parish church – it may be that the same mason was responsible for both sets of decoration.

The windows themselves have been altered over the years. They retain their original shape but instead of the pattern of stone tracery bars that would have divided them, each of the four main windows is divided into two by a single vertical mullion. These probably date from the establishment of the school in the 17th century.

Inside, the chapel is likely to have been originally divided by a screen to define two main areas: a nave for the congregation and a chancel for the priest, as in a parish church. This, and the original fixtures and fittings, have long since disappeared but, bare and altered as it is, the chapel still constitutes a rare and fascinating survival and is crying out to be conserved.

The plan is to restore the chapel by removing additions that were made when it was part of the school during the 19th and 20th centuries. Because it is a solid, well-built structure, less work is needed here than on the Victorian parts of the building which have suffered more deterioration since the school closed in 1988.

The villagers hope that the school will replace their village hall, which is condemned and only has about three years of useful life left. But the restored school will be much more than this. The proposal is for a 'village centre plus' – a facility that will contain computers with internet access, a conference room and other useful features. The Victorian building will lend itself well to such a conversion, and its educational heritage will be reflected in the continuing use of the building for classes for both adults and children. Exhibits showing Pulham's history are also planned, including information on the town's 20th-century claim to fame, when it was home to a base for enormous airships.

The loss of the school and the threatened demise of the village hall are two of the most important issues that face Pulham St Mary today. Restoration will bring a flexible community centre with facilities for everyone, from preschool children to pensioners. There is great local support for the restoration project. Graham King cites a survey in which 90 per cent of respondents expressed a preference for a community use for the building: 'They want access to this important village building – and want to improve what has become an eyesore in the middle of the village,' he adds. The hope is that the restored school will enhance the sense of community in the village, so that Pulham can face the 21st century with some of the optimism that the guild members must have had when they embarked on their new chapel in 1401. ∎

Above left The mouldings and carvings around the chapel doorway have worn over the years, but there is still enough detail to show their quality.

Above right The chapel windows have moulded dripstones with an ornamental carving at either end; this example is a medieval mason's portrait of a lion.

Opposite A pointed doorway in the Gothic style of the 15th century leads into the chapel.

Chedham's Yard

Wellesbourne, Warwickshire

U ntil relatively recently, nearly every village in Britain was home to a number of skilled craftsmen supplying local needs. Carpenters, stonemasons and the like did not travel far to get work. Their workshop – usually referred to simply as their 'shop' – was in the village and most of their customers lived there too. These craftsmen were both manufacturers and repairers, so if you needed a new windowframe or a catch for the door you did not buy it off the shelf – you walked up the road to the village carpenter or metalworker and they would make exactly what you needed.

Mass production, high technology and new patterns in both retailing and industry have changed all that. There are now few village-based traditional craftworkers, and when you do need something specially made the chances are you have to travel a long way, and pay a lot of money, to get it. Some of the crafts, such as wheelwrighting, have almost completely disappeared. Some do survive, like that of the blacksmith who made everything from hinges to horseshoes, but they are thin on the ground.

So any remains of these crafts are important, and the Warwickshire village of Wellesbourne, near Stratford-upon-Avon, is fortunate in that it contains a combined wheelwright's and blacksmith's shop, complete with a vast array of tools and equipment. It survives like a time capsule. The number of tools and other artefacts in these, quite small, buildings is astounding, as project officer Elaine Hughes explains: 'More than 3,000 items have been taken into storage for cataloguing. The people who worked here never threw anything away. Even things that were no longer used might be recycled – this was before the beginning of our disposable society.'

This precious relic, virtually unknown outside the village, is called Chedham's Yard, after the Chedham family who owned and ran the business, one generation after another, until one day in the 1970s when William Chedham completed his last working day, downed tools and closed the door for good. He left behind a unique record – in buildings, tools and ledgers – of a business that had been in his family for about 180 years.

The business seems to have begun in 1813 when Thomas Chedham arrived in Wellesbourne, rented the yard and accommodation from a local man called Edward Riley, and set up in business

"The village of Wellesbourne contains a combined wheelwright's and blacksmith's shop, complete with a vast array of tools and equipment. It survives like a time capsule."

Opposite In the forge at Chedham's Yard a host of tongs and other metalworking tools hang above a pair of anvils.

Above Making and repairing cartwheels was one of the main activities at Chedham's Yard.

Village Voice

"You know, it was always a busy place in those days. There used to be a line of old carts and wagons and things lined up right into the street waiting to be seen to. They used to have the saw bench up there where the gate is now. They used to get some fair-sized trees and it all had to be man-handled, there was no lifting gear or anything."

BILL CHEDHAM Wellesbourne

as a wheelwright. A few years later he had started a smithy and was a blacksmith too, and by 1850 records show a small group of buildings on the site, just as there are today.

Life in the countryside, which seems so slow to change, is in fact rarely straightforward or secure. Thomas Chedham's business seems to have gone through rough patches in the 1840s and 1850s, with Thomas twice declared bankrupt. But somehow he managed to hang on to the yard and by the 1870s and 1880s, when Henry Chedham was running the business, the owner's three sons and several staff were employed there – there must have been plenty of work for them all.

It was in this period also that Wellesbourne achieved its main claim to fame. In 1872 Joseph Arch, a farm worker and Methodist lay preacher from nearby Barford, called a meeting at the Stag's Head public house, a short walk from Chedham's Yard. Arch addressed a large crowd of agricultural workers as part of a struggle to improve working conditions on Britain's farms. The main result of the meeting was the foundation of the National Agricultural Workers' Union, bringing for the first time the strength and protection of a union to the thousands of people who relied on the land for their livelihood. The Chedhams, with their agriculturally based business, were probably at the meeting.

The Chedhams' business seems to have survived by being adaptable. Its core work was making wheels for carts and carriages and various metalworking tasks including, probably, shoeing horses. There would have been plenty of demand for wheels and other items relating to transport, because by the early 19th century Wellesbourne stood at the centre of the local turnpike road network and the local gentry regularly visited the village during the hunting season. The Mordaunt family at nearby Walton Hall, their ancestral home, would have been regular customers, as would the many local farmers round about.

Surviving documents from between 1868 and 1882 give a valuable insight into the kind of business the Chedham family were doing. Their main income was from repairing wagons and from renting out a threshing machine to local farmers. As well as metalworking and wheel-making, the yard undertook general woodwork, sawing, painting and signwriting. As workers who combined skills with both metal and wood

they could repair just about anything on the farm – ledger entries record repairs to pig troughs, wheelbarrows, wagons, carts, carriages, water wheels, ploughs, saws and a host of other implements. People rarely threw things away when they could take them to the yard for repair.

The precious remains of all this activity are contained in a group of brick-built and wooden buildings. The blacksmith's shop – brick-walled, cobble-floored and with a roof of clay tiles – is one of the most evocative. It contains two forges, each with leather bellows, and a pair of anvils – one small (probably for items such as horseshoes) and one heavier, in the traditional shape with flat face and 'nose'. The fact that there are two forges is significant; it confirms the notion that the yard had periods when there was a lot of work. The blacksmith's shop is littered with tools, which take up every available surface and hang from nails on the roof beams. There is every implement a craft-worker would have

Above Boards bearing the names of wagon owners hang on one wall.

Left A vast collection of tools and metal artefacts surrounds the bellows in the forge.

Opposite Ivy trails its way around the fragile structure, concealing walls and window frames that are in need of repair.

needed to shape the heated metal into anything from pokers, hinges and latches, to fittings for carts and wagons.

The other main building is the wheelwright's shop. This is another brick and tiled structure with a floor of packed earth, this time home to a vast assembly of woodworking tools. All this equipment was used in conjunction with machinery in the yard, for example there is a tyring platform and tyre-bending machine that were used to fit iron hoops or tyres around wooden wheels. There is also a saw bench for cutting timber (originally powered by a small steam engine) together with a place that may once have housed a sawpit where two men would have worked a huge handsaw; one standing in the pit and the other at ground level, alternately pushing and pulling the saw to cut the timber into planks.

The planks were stacked in the drying shed, an open-sided structure which now contains some remains of the Chedhams' threshing machine together with several wheels and a handcart, presumably made by the family. Another of the Chedhams' carts is preserved in the Shakespeare Countryside Museum at the house of Mary Arden (Shakespeare's mother) near Stratford.

All this is contained in and around a set of buildings that are now in a dire state of disrepair. The site gives an impression of neglect, overgrown as it is with ivy and weeds, but its problems go much deeper than this. Most of the buildings are in a dangerous condition – public access is currently out of the question. Elaine Hughes explains the reasons for this: 'It was an ad hoc construction, and the buildings were put up quickly as the need arose, and altered as the needs changed. There are no deep foundations – most of the walls just go a couple of bricks into the ground.' So these fragile walls will have to be restored with the utmost care. It is a daunting job, but this is not a big site and it will be worth the effort to make the workshops safe and sound for another century or more.

There is also the challenge of the contents. Many of these also need restoration but before this can happen the machines, tools and other remains need to be properly catalogued. This task has already begun and the professionals who are carrying out the work have already removed some of the items to secure storage. When the buildings are restored they can be brought back to make the yard into a comprehensively stocked,

living museum, working forge and educational resource. It is hoped that the crafts of wheelwrighting and smithing will once more be practised here and that people will be able to learn at various levels about these once-common crafts. There is vast potential for schools and for adults who want to learn craft skills, and for collaboration with the local agricultural college which already runs courses for blacksmiths.

The restoration of the yard would mean a great deal for the village of Wellesbourne. The parish council bought the site in 1992 on the basis that it should be preserved. All are keen that this very special survival of Wellesbourne's working past should be kept for the future. ▪

Opposite Two views of the tool collection at Chedham's Yard: a range of chisels and a variety of files, pincers and gouges.

Below A round jig in the yard was used to hold cartwheels so that metal tyres could be fitted.

Bottom Some of the woodwork is showing the effects of time, the weather and algae.

Pennoyer's School

North

The North of England, the region that stretches from Lancashire and Yorkshire northwards to the Scottish border, is an area of many aspects. Two sides of it are best known: its big industrial and mercantile cities, from Liverpool and Manchester to Bradford and Newcastle; and its vast unspoilt tracts of beautiful countryside, such as the Cheviots, the North York Moors and the Lake District. In both city and country, the North is one of the richest and most rewarding regions of all.

In areas like the North York Moors you can go for miles without passing through a village, but the North does have plenty of villages and they take many forms. There are picturesque settlements, home to farming communities like some of those in the Yorkshire Dales that look as if they have hardly changed in 200 years; estate villages, once occupied by the workers in country houses and their farms; and coastal settlements that were once rich through fishing.

Travelling through this large region you are struck by the local differences in building materials, particularly the large variety of building stones. This means that the walls of the North's traditional buildings – cottages, farmhouses, barns and so on – come in all sorts of colours: dark gritstone in parts of Lancashire, green slate in Cumbria, red sandstone in North Yorkshire. The palette is more varied still because in some regions many of the houses are traditionally whitewashed or colour-washed.

HIGHERFORD MILL
Higherford, Lancashire

HEUGH GUN BATTERY
Hartlepool

The rural landscape is punctuated with many other building types too. The North is famous for its abbeys, built for medieval monks who liked the isolation of the rural northern counties and who benefited from farming the area's sheep pastures. There are also many medieval castles, strongholds of lords of the manor and of families who needed to protect themselves from cross-border raiders from Scotland.

And then there are the industrial villages. The North, with its textile mills, was one of the engines of the British economy in the Victorian period. Much of this manufacturing took place in towns but the villages contributed their fair share; there had been rural textile workers long before the industrial revolution made big mills and factories a reality in the 18th century. In the Middle Ages the North was a major wool-producing area and many of the fleeces that came off the backs of Yorkshire sheep were spun and woven into cloth in local villages by people working at home. The north west became famous for its cotton production and in some villages – mostly in Lancashire but in Yorkshire too – there are still cottages with big upstairs windows that let in extra light for the weavers who produced cloth there.

When large-scale industry arrived, some of the factories and textile mills were built in villages. Many were built of stone and, although they were big buildings, they blended quite well into the village scene and the landscape beyond. But soon after the Second World War this old industry, like many other manufacturing businesses, hit hard times. The development of newer fabrics such as nylon and its derivatives, together with cheap imports, meant that the cotton mills stopped making a profit and slowly but surely most of them closed. This decline, combined with the demise of other industries – from steel-working to ship-building – was a hard blow to the North's towns and villages alike. While former mill-workers looked for new work, the mill buildings stood empty and, in many cases, began to fall into dilapidation.

This change has meant that the North has had to regroup, and it has sometimes been a painful process. There has been a huge effort to regenerate the cities, as booming Newcastle and Manchester demonstrate. But in the countryside, where poverty is more scattered and quick fixes are more difficult, there is still work to do. And with around four-fifths of this region's land being rural the job is challenging.

One solution has been to develop the tourism industry. In most of the region tourism now accounts for around 10 per cent of jobs, and the North has a prime asset in the Lake District – not to mention areas of outstanding natural beauty such as the Cheviots and the Yorkshire Dales. There have been other changes in the economy, too. There has been a large-scale move away from

Left to right The masonry at each of the North's restoration candidate buildings produces a characteristic texture. At Howsham Mill the walls are faced with large stone blocks, with still bigger stones in an alternating 'long and short' pattern at the corners; Higherford Mill has smaller blocks; at Heugh Gun Battery there is an outer covering of concrete.

the old heavy industries and textile manufacturing towards creative and computer-based businesses, environmental technology, financial services and other 'modern' occupations. All these are businesses that can, at least in part, take place in rural areas and so they have the potential to benefit the village communities of the North as well as the region's newly burgeoning cities. And some of the new businesses have found homes in the old mills, which have proved to be highly versatile buildings with big, flexible spaces that can be put to all sorts of new uses.

Two of the North's restoration candidates have their origins in the industrial past and look towards a very different future. Yorkshire's Howsham Mill was a small-scale local flour mill, of the kind that existed all over the region before the industrial revolution – but it is a small mill with a difference because it was built in a highly ornate, 18th-century style, to improve the view on a country estate. Lancashire's Higherford Mill is completely different, a large-scale industrial complex with vast weaving sheds built in the latest factory style during the first half of the 19th century. It is quite clearly a purely utilitarian building but nevertheless it has an austere beauty of its own.

Both of these buildings were once, in their different ways, lynchpins of their respective communities, and they have the chance to be so

once more. Howsham Mill, in its isolated country setting, could become a visitor centre where people could learn about the history and environment of the area. Higherford has already become a centre where creative artists and craftspeople produce and sell their wares; with further restoration it could do this work still more effectively and on a larger scale.

The third northern restoration candidate, the Heugh Gun Battery near Hartlepool, is a very different building. It is a reminder of the role of the region in wartime, especially during the First World War when it was attacked from the sea, but also still earlier, when Britain was threatened by French invasion in the 19th century. It is already in active use, hosting living history and other events that inform and educate the public about this aspect of the history of the north east. Restoration will enable the battery's custodians to extend this work, bringing more visitors to the area and benefiting the wider community.

The North has long been proud of its heritage and culture, and all these buildings have their loyal and enthusiastic supporters. They are all unique, but they point the way forward for other similar heritage projects in the region, projects in which the saving of an old building can combine with a viable future use that benefits local people and showcases the creativity of this most vibrant of English regions. ▨

Howsham Mill
Howsham, North Yorkshire

"Howsham Mill is a rather isolated building, standing alone on its island on a country estate, but it was once at the heart of community life."

Water mills are among our most fascinating working buildings. Both their structure and their machinery can tell us much about the industrial past that made Britain great. Mill design and engineering, so important to the prosperity of manufacturers and to the daily lives of working people, was usually the responsibility of unknown local men – millwrights who became highly skilled in devising machinery that could convert the movement of running water into power, which could turn millstones to grind corn into flour, or drive industrial machinery.

Water mills are therefore interesting buildings, but rarely beautiful. But Howsham Mill, a small structure set on an island in the River Derwent about 10 miles north-east of York, is an exception to this rule. As well as being interesting historically it is also visually stunning, even though its unusual decorative façades are already in a sad state of decay.

Howsham Mill was built in the late 1750s – the date 1760 is carved above the entrance. Apparently there was already a mill on the site but it is not known how old it was. Whatever it looked like, the 1760 mill was no doubt a transformation, because it is built in the most ornate Gothic style. This style of architecture – featuring pointed arches and often elaborate carved decoration – was fashionable in the Middle Ages and is seen in countless churches and cathedrals. In the mid-18th century the Gothic style, which had by then been out of favour for more than 200 years, was revived and once more became highly fashionable.

The new popularity of Gothic was partly the result of the work of Horace Walpole, whose Gothic-style house, Strawberry Hill in Twickenham, was featured in the previous series of *Restoration*. Walpole started to remodel his house in the Gothic idiom between 1747 and 1753; Howsham Mill is therefore a very early example of Gothic Revival architecture. We do not know for sure who designed it but it was likely to have been John Carr of York, a successful architect who was active for much of the second

Opposite The site of the waterwheel can be seen though this brick archway.

Below The stone-faced front of the mill has a series of pointed Gothic openings.

Top A broken millstone is turned up to show how its face is cut with grooves.

Above Parts of the mill mechanism, such as this gear wheel, still survive on the site.

half of the 18th century and who designed many public buildings and country houses in Yorkshire and neighbouring counties.

Carr, or whoever did design Howsham Mill, pulled out all the Gothic stops. There were pairs of pointed windows on each of the main façades and above these were placed intricate little quatrefoil (four-lobed) windows. In the centre of each side was either a pointed doorway or another window. And the whole composition was topped by little pinnacles that would not have looked too out of place on a medieval parish church or cathedral. James Williams, an inspector for the Royal Commission on Historic Monuments, described the mill as, 'of great architectural interest...a very rare example of the Gothic Revival style as applied to a functional building'.

This extraordinarily elaborate design tells us that Howsham Mill was meant to be more than simply functional. It was also an 'eye-catcher', a building intended to form an ornamental feature in itself. Eye-catchers were quite popular in the landscape gardens of 18th-century England and, instead of building a mill that intruded on the view, Carr produced one that was an eye-catcher too. To create such landscapes, entire villages were sometimes swept away. Howsham survived, but only just – some of the houses were removed when the park was laid out so the village shrank and changed shape.

Howsham Mill is a rather isolated building, standing alone on its little island on a country estate, but it was once at the heart of community life. In the 18th and 19th centuries country houses were the economic engines of the rural economy. Dozens of people worked in them, scores more toiled in the fields around about, still more worked in outlying properties like Howsham Mill. Such estates, owned by the landed few, provided a living and a home for the many. So, although built by the gentry and at least partly an ornamental structure, the mill played as vital a part in rural life as many a more typical village building.

The landed family who built this remarkable structure were the Cholmleys, the first of whom, Nathaniel Cholmley, inherited Howsham Hall and its estate in 1755 from his relatives in the Wentworth family. The house itself is a Jacobean building with an exterior still very much as it was when it was built in around 1619. But if the Cholmleys did not want to replace their house they were keen to improve the grounds, and the mill, which must have been begun soon after they arrived, is an important result of this.

As the estate passed from one member of the Cholmley family to another the mill continued to turn. In 1839–40 it was insured for £300 and may have been refitted at this time – it was clearly a valuable asset to the estate. During this period the millers were members of the Wilson-Remmer family, who had run the mill on behalf of the Cholmleys for several generations. By 1903 the Wilson-Remmers had taken over the mill and were renting it from the Cholmleys, but the business did not pay well and was soon passed on to other hands. The wheel continued to operate until the late 1940s, by which time Howsham Hall was standing empty and was threatened with demolition. The Hall was saved, becoming a school, but by the 1950s there was no economic role for a water mill and Howsham Mill was finally abandoned to time and the elements.

At this point the mill began a downward spiral of decay that is all too familiar where buildings at risk are concerned. The interior was looted and equipment removed for its scrap value. Trees and shrubs attacked the delicate fabric of the walls. Slates came off and roof beams began to rot. Vandals set a fire inside, damaging both contents and structural timbers. Rain and frost began to eat away at the ornate stonework of the walls.

Left The mill's custodians know the importance of preserving original materials and these bricks have been cleaned and stacked, for use when the building is restored.

Below The Gothic openings are topped with neatly cut dripstones. Even in the 18th century, 'antique' details like these were more often seen on churches and country houses than on industrial buildings.

At one point during the 1960s it looked as if the building would be demolished, but it survived to be listed and eventually to be put on the *Buildings at Risk Register*. In spite of the added attacks of weather and arsonists, the walls, together with some of the roof timbers and part of the mechanism, have hung on. It is still possible to appreciate the beauty of this remarkable building, fragile and damaged as it is.

Village Voice

"Howsham has no central meeting place or village hall, so the mill could be a great resource for the village. And many local people have already given their support, either in words or with practical help in clearing the site."

MO MACLEOD Howsham

Mo MacLeod who, with her husband David Mann, bought the mill in 1994 with the hope of restoring it, saw from the outset the importance of involving the local community: 'As people who were new to the area we talked to everyone in the neighbourhood about our plans for the mill. They were incredibly supportive and many joined us in our efforts to cut back the vegetation and clear the site.' But Mo MacLeod realised that, even with all this help, it was too big a project for individuals to tackle. The mill is now owned by the Renewable Heritage Trust, which is actively working towards restoring the building and giving it a new life.

Howsham Mill is worth restoring for itself, as a building of outstanding beauty that could again become an asset to the landscape. Although lacking a roof, its walls are surprisingly solid and, as Mo MacLeod explains, many elements have been preserved: 'When we tidied up the site we kept many stones, bricks and slates that belonged to the structure, in the hope that we will be able to put them back where they belong.'

But the plans for restoration go far beyond bricks and mortar. The Renewable Heritage Trust has a vision that the mill can become a showcase for environmental sustainability. So when the water wheel turns again, the power it produces will be used to generate electricity. It is hoped that revenue from selling the electricity to the national grid will be used to fund future conservation projects and any repairs the building needs. In addition, the mill will become an educational resource centre, promoting the use of renewable energy and advocating a more sustainable way of life. A transparent walkway above the wheel, enabling visitors to see exactly how it works, is one possibility.

Further, the project will foster education about the local natural environment, enabling people to come to study the area's geology and wildlife, including the unspoilt woodland and otter habitats, which the scheme also aims to conserve. Displays on local wildlife could be combined with historical information to give visitors an intriguing picture of the village and the area, past and present. And the trustees have also been working with other organisations, including a group that provides courses on traditional skills such as willow-weaving and bench-making, and with the Youth Hostels Association, with a view to providing accommodation in part of the mill building.

There are many different possibilities and the trustees are developing a range of ideas that fit in with both the mill's history and its environment. Whichever options are finally chosen, they will ensure a valuable future for what promises to be a flagship project, with benefits ranging from sustainability to education. It is hoped that the building will once more become a genuine local asset. ▪

Opposite A view across the wheel pit shows how the shaft passes through a neat brick arch into the mill building itself.

Below A ruined site like Howsham Mill yields many treasures. Bottles left over from some Victorian or early 20th-century worker's lunch compete for attention with architectural fragments, such as a piece of stone carved with this double-curved, or ogee, moulding.

Higherford Mill
Higherford, Lancashire

Opposite Higherford Mill's central block, with its broad-arched entrance, rises three storeys. Round-headed windows give a touch of grandeur to the front that faces the road. The low wall to the right conceals one of the weaving sheds.

Below The date 1832, carved in one of the stone blocks, marks one of the many alterations to the building since its construction in the 1820s.

The North is famous for its large textile mills, which transformed British industry and the working lives of millions of people in the 19th century. The textile industry changed the face of the North's towns, but it also had a profound effect on its rural communities, elevating small, isolated hamlets into major centres of manufacturing. The Pendle area in Lancashire is one region that was affected profoundly by the textile business, and one of the most important survivals of this development is Higherford Mill.

Higherford Mill was originally built in 1824 and was powered by water. The owner was Thomas Grimshaw and his family ran the mill, sometimes in partnership with others, for almost 50 years. But 20 years into this period disaster struck: a fire engulfed the building and the mill had to be rebuilt, almost from scratch. This was the first of a series of transformations that saw the mill grow and develop with changing technology. The building embodies the developing industry, powered first by a water wheel, then by steam, and finally by electricity. This history of change is one of the things that makes Higherford Mill special.

Higherford was a weaving mill that produced cotton cloth and was part of a vast trading network which owed its success to Britain's enormous empire. The raw cotton was brought from India to Lancashire where it was spun into thread and woven into cloth. The finished product was then sold worldwide. Weaving had been a speciality in the north of England for hundreds of years, developing as part of the wool trade and adapting itself successfully when cotton importing began. To begin with it was a business based on homeworkers using handlooms, but by the 1820s, when Higherford was built, it had become a large-scale industry

"The textile industry changed the face of the North's towns, but it also had a profound effect on its rural communities, elevating small isolated hamlets into major centres of manufacturing."

Village Voice

"By taking time there is more chance that the project will take root in the community. At the beginning many local people were unsure about the benefits of restoring the mill. But we talked to them about the importance of mills in the area and explained the project and the drawbacks of pulling the mill down. And the community came round – now everyone is behind the project."

JOHN MILLER Higherford Mill

with rows of power looms in large mills producing cloth by the acre.

Most local mills were originally powered by water; a study of 1984 identified 34 mills in Pendle that began with water power and there were many others in neighbouring areas, too. But few of these retain any obvious evidence of this phase of their existence. The wholesale change to steam power had in general happened by the middle of the 19th century and, if a mill survived into the 20th century, electricity would take over, in turn sweeping away the steam engine. With so many mills converted to other uses after the 20th-century decline in the textile industry, still more of this early heritage was destroyed.

But Higherford is different. Here, many of the features associated with the first, water-powered phase, remain. When the fire struck in 1844, the wheel pit and waterwheel survived and these were incorporated into the rebuilt mill. A weir and sluice up the valley fed water into a leat or channel, which in turn led to the mill's wheel pit with its overshot waterwheel. Much of this arrangement also survives, although the wheel itself has gone. One aim of the restoration project is to make the most of these survivals by building a new waterwheel, so that visitors can see at first hand how the mill was originally powered.

As they watch the machinery turn they will be appreciating the fruits of another important local industry – the business of making mill machinery. In the 19th century the Pendle area was home to a number of factories making everything from bobbins and shuttles, through whole looms and loom components, to steam engines. One local man, John Pilling, began making hand looms before developing the Lancashire power loom, which he produced at his factory by the Colne Water, not far from Higherford Mill. Another manufacturer, William Bell White of the Red Scar Works, started with spindles before going on to full-scale loom-making in the early decades of the 20th century. Factories like these show how the textile business dominated the entire local economy.

To harness the power from the rushing water and from the later steam and electric power plants, Higherford had banks of looms housed in two enormous weaving sheds. When you approach the mill from the road these are not the most obvious parts of the building. The tall central block, with its rows of windows – arched

at the front for an effect of extra grandeur, rectangular and utilitarian at the sides – dominates the site. But on either side stretch the two large, low weaving sheds.

At first sight there is something odd about these sheds. Weaving is a process that requires plenty of light – you need to be able to see the threads – but Higherford's sheds seem to have no windows. This is because they are lit from above, with glazing in the roof. The sheds are in fact a very early example of a kind of building that became common all over industrial Lancashire during the 19th century, the 'north-lit' shed. The roof is made up of a series of ridges and one side of each ridge is glazed, so that light floods into the interior.

By the end of the century thousands of acres of Lancashire factory space were roofed in this way, and the design was spreading all over Britain. Soon, not just weaving sheds but all kinds of factories had north-lit roofs as industrialists everywhere caught on to the advantages of plentiful natural light. The resulting large, well-lit spaces are ideal for all sorts of activities. But

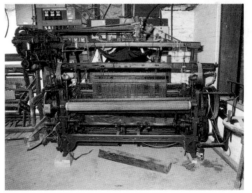

there is a problem with roofs like this. Their shape can make maintenance access difficult and, if they are not maintained, water can penetrate the many valleys, rotting the supporting timbers beneath. This is one of the conservation challenges that has been faced at Higherford Mill.

The mill seems to have prospered in the late 19th century, when it was owned by the Wiseman family. The Wisemans extended the buildings in the 1880s, taking down the old engine house and

Above One of the magnificent north-lit weaving-shed roofs still awaits restoration. Maintenance has always been a challenge with these delicate structures.

Left A surviving loom stands as tribute to the mill's long history of cloth production.

Opposite A view across one of the weaving-shed roofs shows some of Higherford's other buildings, a mixture of stone, slate and whitewash.

installing a new power plant, boiler house and other buildings. The Wisemans continued to operate the mill until the 1950s, by which time the cotton industry was in decline and production at Higherford was slowing. Although space in the mill was leased to another company in the 1960s, by 1969 the mill had closed. It was saved from demolition when it was bought by the Lancashire Heritage Trust, now part of the Heritage Trust for the North West.

It is a big project and progress so far has been steady but John Miller, chief executive of the Heritage Trust for the North West, stresses the benefits of not moving too fast. Working at a steady pace has given the Trust time to introduce the local community to the project and get people on board. It has also enabled them to confront the building's problems one by one.

The Trust has had to face a number of challenges in their work to save the mill. Because the structure was built to allow water to flow through it, water damage to some of the masonry was a problem. The ridged roofs of the weaving sheds, with many rotten timbers, were in pressing need of restoration, and widespread repointing was required. The good news is that some of this work has already been done. The Trust has completed Phase 1 of the work, involving structural repairs, restoration of one of the shed roofs, and the creation of artists' workshops in part of the mill. Phase 2 is underway, and will provide more working units and a reception area.

But there is still much to do to complete the transformation of the building into both a centre for creative enterprise and a unique visitor attraction. The Trust has identified a number of projects that need to be completed, including the restoration of a waterwheel, repair of the various water tunnels, channels and sluices, various repointing works, the repair of the roof of the south shed, and the installation of a glass floor so that visitors can see the workings of the mill.

The finished project will be beneficial in all sorts of ways. The building, housing local creative artists, will enable these tenants both to work and to sell their products directly to the public. There will also be spaces for exhibitions, classes and creative workshops, and special events so there will be huge creative gains. There will also be educational benefits to those who come to look at the restored mill and its

machinery. The building will work in conjunction with the nearby restored Pendle Heritage Centre to achieve this aim. As John Miller points out: 'Conservation has led to regeneration in this area already and it is continuing to do so with this project.' In addition, there will be economic advantages ranging from employment opportunities to the creation of a visitor attraction that will benefit the wider local economy.

The Trust is aware of the importance of making the building sustainable, by using recycled materials, keeping heating costs down and ensuring that there is an income to keep the place going. Higherford Mill should be a hive of activity for years to come. ▩

Opposite Sluice gates (*above*) and a stone arch (*below*) form part of the system of channels that delivered water to the mill's wheel: but the close proximity of water has threatened the building's structure.

Below The mill's interiors are beautifully light, especially in the top-lit weaving sheds. The impressive roofs give generous areas of working space.

Heugh Gun Battery
Hartlepool

For much of the 19th century Britain was under threat of invasion. From 1805 to 1815 the Napoleonic Wars pitted Britain and her allies against France, and a ring of coastal defences was built to protect the island from possible attacks. But the animosity did not end with the conclusion of the Napoleonic Wars. Repeated threats of invasion meant that the British army had to keep their coastal forts manned and continuously developing military technology, from ironclad battleships to rifled guns, meant that these fortifications often needed upgrading. For much of the Victorian period it made sense to talk about 'fortress Britain'.

In the 20th century there were new threats, such as the big ship-borne guns of the First World War and the merciless aerial bombardments of the Second. So Britain's ageing ring of forts, ramparts and gun batteries

was adapted and pressed into service once more. Naturally, the major strategic sites were especially well defended – the great naval bases of the south coast and the Thames estuary approach to London were protected by huge forts – but there were also defences on key headlands and near smaller towns. One of the most interesting is Heugh Gun Battery, on the headland near the port and ship-building centre of Hartlepool on the north-east coast.

The story began in the 1850s. Gun emplacements were set up to defend Hartlepool in 1855: one at the lighthouse facing east across Tees Bay, the other at Fairy Cove on the northern edge of the headland. In 1859–60 these positions were upgraded with the addition of the new Heugh Battery. The structure took just under a year to build and involved the sealing of ancient caves beneath the site – an essential measure to guard against subsidence. The new battery was positioned between the two existing gun positions, and the three combined positions were designed to provide a formidable arc of fire at any enemy ships approaching the headland.

The next few decades saw the battery manned and continuously upgraded. In the 1880s, for example, the positions were equipped with new 64-pounder, rifled muzzle-loading guns, which were more accurate than their old 68-pounder guns. With these superior weapons the battery needed three rather than the original four emplacements, so one emplacement was filled in.

The most dramatic upgrade, however, came when the battery was virtually completely rebuilt in 1899–1900. Most of the old buildings were demolished and two circular gun emplacements of mass concrete were erected, together with a brick-lined magazine complex, a new command

"Heugh Battery faced the beginning of the First World War strong and well equipped, and this turned out to be just as well. By December 1914 it was becoming clear that the hoped-for early end to the First World War was not going to come."

Above The brick-built barrack and stores building is currently used to house the equipment and materials used to maintain and repair the battery complex.

post and troop facilities including barracks, cookhouse, stores and workshops. In around 1913 there was a different form of improvement – a camouflage screen. This took the form of a row of wooden slats along the back of the battery wall, cut to look like a broken urban skyline from a distance, making the battery much harder to see from the water. The screen has recently been recreated and is still very effective when the battery is viewed from out at sea.

So Heugh Battery faced the beginning of the First World War strong and well equipped, and this turned out to be just as well. By December 1914 it was becoming clear that the hoped-for early end to the First World War was not going to come. The two sides were locked in conflict and the Germans were daunted by the strength of the British Navy. They decided to try to weaken it by attacking targets on the British coast, hoping that navy ships would be sent to defend these threatened positions and that, thus dispersed across a wide area, the British fleet could then be picked off a bit at a time. One of the targets was Hartlepool, a good place to attack because of its ship-building industry, and three German warships arrived off the coast on 16 December 1914. It was a misty morning and the German ships sailed closer to the shore than they had intended before unleashing a bombardment at the battery. Because of their proximity their shells were not as effective against the fortifications as they should have been and, although there were many casualties, the battery itself survived – many of the German shells bounced off before exploding further inland, killing locals and destroying civilian buildings in the process.

Meanwhile, the men in the Heugh Battery were responding, and took full advantage of the enemy ships' close range. The battery's guns did enough damage to force the ships to withdraw,

Village Voice

"There's tremendous interest locally in the battery. Most local people are behind the project and many came to help on day one. There's also a team of World War I re-enactors who keep the place alive."

JOHN SOUTHCOTE Heugh Battery

but not before there had been many deaths on both sides. John Southcote, a local man who has long been closely involved in the restoration of the battery, describes what this meant to the defenders: 'These were men who had been until recently part-time territorial soldiers manning the battery. Now they had joined the regular army and they were fighting for their lives and their homes, because most of them lived close by.'

Although some locals, including a group of cockle-pickers, continued going stoically about their business, many of those who lived or worked near the coast were soon retreating inland – in some cases taking their Christmas cakes with them – leaving behind many damaged buildings and a destroyed gasworks that had left the town without heat and light.

But without the firepower of the Heugh Battery and the bravery of its men, things would have been much worse. Soon the people who had fled came back and joined the rest of those in the

town, and their fighting spirit ensured that a clearing-up operation was soon under way. The enemy ships were sent packing and Heugh remained the only British battery to engage enemy ships for the entire war.

After this dramatic episode, the authorities took steps to make Hartlepool still better defended. New batteries were set up on the old pier (now known as the Pilot Pier) and on nearby Spion Kop, and the lighthouse was taken down to give an uninterrupted arc of fire. But never again did the Heugh Battery have to face the challenge it did on that misty morning in December 1914.

The battery was altered yet again during the Second World War. Its defences were extended, one of the emplacements was enlarged and a trench was dug to reach the troops' and gunners' accommodation. Extra buildings, including a cookhouse and plotting room, were also added. By now, of course, the main danger was from the air, although there was still the possibility of a

Above From a few hundred yards away the low-lying structures of the battery are virtually invisible. From still further away, the jagged-topped wall looks like the roofs of houses on a skyline.

Opposite below The rear of the battery command post shows the external stairs rising to the top of the concrete structure. In the stone wall below is part of the 1860 powder magazine.

seaborne attack. By 1942 the Luftwaffe was regularly bombing Hartlepool so a dual-purpose gun was installed.

But the bombing did not last long. By 1944, with the focus of the war shifted to mainland Europe, the battery was kept on a 'care and maintenance' basis and many of the troops were moved elsewhere. For some years in the post-war period it became an important training location before being decommissioned in 1956. Since then the site has been home to a sports centre, a community arts project and a car park. Meanwhile, various military structures such as the kitchen and NCO room to the north of the barrack block have been demolished, together with the lighthouse battery.

Enough of the structure remains, though, to bring the battery back to life. The two gun emplacements are still there, surrounded with concrete and a defensive earthwork to shield them from attack, just as they were during the two world wars. Beneath them is the underground magazine, lined in whitewashed brick and still containing its shell lift. Overlooking the emplacements – and looking out to sea – is the battery command post, a stark structure that abuts the original powder magazine of 1859–60. Nearby is a brick barrack room and administration building. Taken together, these surviving structures give a good idea of what the place was like during the First and Second World Wars. And the site is often brought to life, as the result of the activities of an enthusiastic and knowledgeable body of local historians, re-enactors and other volunteers. As John Southcote explains: 'The volunteers make it. There is a sizeable body of people of all ages, from retired bank managers to carpenters, who volunteer here. There's tremendous interest locally and of course the residents in the nearby houses are pleased that the battery is used and is no longer a target for vandals and trouble-makers.'

Already around 1,750 visitors a year enjoy coming to Heugh Battery, but a restored battery could attract many more. The Heugh Battery Trust hopes to refurbish the rear block as a visitor centre, restore the underground magazines and level the main open spaces so they are safe to walk on. Multimedia points and other innovative displays will give visitors more information, and re-enactments will continue. Training will also be on offer for those who want to learn restoration skills and apply them to other buildings.

The Trust is not only aware of the huge tourist potential of the site, but is also keen to stress its educational value. It is an obvious resource for the history curriculum, but there is also potential for schools to use it in their work in art and design, science, geography and drama. The battery had a huge impact on north-east England during wartime. Now it has the chance to extend its influence in more peaceful ways. ▪

Opposite The battery's magazine is lined and vaulted in whitewashed brick.

Above left The battery boasts several impressive pieces of artillery, including this 5.5-inch gun.

Above right A simple concrete name-plaque is set in one of the brick walls.

Higherford Mill

Howsham Mill

Heugh Gun Battery

Wales

Apart from the 2.9 million or so who live there, few people know Wales well, yet it is characterised with clichés – pit villages, chapels, scrum-halfs and male voice choirs – and justly famous for its scenery of course, especially the mountains of Snowdonia.

The landscape it is not all mountainous, and for a small country Wales has a great variety of scenery. There are large areas of delightful, and delightfully empty, hilly green country in mid-Wales, a quiet landscape punctuated by isolated farmsteads, sheep folds, deserted mine buildings and abandoned chapels. There are smaller highlights too, such as the purple moors of Hiraethog in the north-east, Pembrokeshire's Preseli Hills, where sheep farmers raise their animals on the remains of ancient mountains, and the green border country marked by Offa's Dyke. And Wales, like the rest of the United Kingdom, has its share of beautiful islands. Those off the south-west coast are renowned for their craggy terrain, colonies of seabirds and archaeological remains from the Bronze Age and the early Christian periods.

A rich variety of buildings complements this diverse landscape. For example, there is a strong tradition of timber building in the border country of eastern Wales, while clay is a common material in the west. Elsewhere, there are still lots of traditional stone buildings – not only houses but an array of barns and other farm buildings too. The stones range from the pinkish sandstone of

PEN YR ORSEDD QUARRY
Nantlle, Caernarfon

PRICHARD JONES INSTITUTE
Newborough, Anglesey

south-west Wales to the grey slates of the north. Many of these farm buildings are fascinating but many are also endangered because changes in agricultural methods have rendered them redundant. Add to these a heritage of industrial buildings (again, many either falling down or looking for a new use after the decline of the various kinds of mining once pursued in Wales) and the result is an environment of great richness.

So there is much more to Wales than scenery and industry; the country has changed and is still changing. In the second half of the 20th century Wales suffered more than most regions from the decline of mining and heavy industry – the coal mines were closing, exhausted or uneconomic in a climate of privately owned pits, and other traditional Welsh industries, such as steel production and manufacturing, were also in freefall. The Welsh found themselves with high unemployment and widespread poverty.

This decline had a massive impact in south Wales in particular. This is the most industrialised part of the country and the traditionally close-knit communities of the valleys began to disintegrate. But the rest of Wales was affected too. While the rural areas came under the same pressures felt in farming regions all over Britain, there were also pockets of industry that had to adapt or perish. The slate mines and quarries in the north were a case in point, with closures leaving a scarred landscape and a bereft workforce. And as the jobs disappeared the traditional social centres of chapel and miners' institute also declined.

In the Victorian period Welsh coal had fuelled the nation's industry and Welsh slate had covered the roofs of houses across Britain and beyond. Now Wales found itself marginalised industrially and economically. But the Welsh have fought back. Devolution has brought more investment and patterns of work and life are changing. Living standards have risen, more job opportunities have opened up and for many people life is better.

In rural areas, though, there are still big challenges. Farming is as tough here as anywhere and because Wales has a large population living in the countryside, where earnings tend to be lower, average incomes are still generally lower in Wales than in most areas of England. Not all the solutions to this problem are economic. One result of these difficulties, for example, has been a tendency to value more greatly what is unique about the place. So there has been a resurgence of Welsh culture in the rural areas of north and west Wales. Plaid Cymru, the old nationalist party, has gained particular strength in rural areas, use of the Welsh language has increased here and Welsh-speaking schools have flourished. The Welsh are still a stateless people, but they have guarded their identity.

The fields of heritage and conservation have helped this process and will continue to do so, a fact that is borne out by the Welsh candidates in this series of *Restoration*. One, a village institute in Newborough, Anglesey, where local people could gather for both entertainment and education, goes right to the heart of Welsh culture. There were institutes all over Wales in the early 20th century but many have disappeared as better transport has enabled people to seek entertainment farther from home. But this tendency to decamp to the local town or city in the evenings means that people scatter and the old social cohesion of the institute, where a whole community could gather and have fun, is often sorely missed.

The other two restoration candidates, the Pen Yr Orsedd slate mine in north Wales and Pembrey Court in the south-west, represent different aspects of the country. They are both typical of their regions, the court with its stone walls and the mine buildings partly made of the slate that was extracted nearby. They are also both typical country buildings in that they are relatively simple structures. At first glance this makes them rather forbidding – and daunting candidates for a new use. But in fact such buildings are ideal candidates for new roles as they contain

generous, flexible spaces that can be used in a variety of ways. Like the institute, they also offer hope for social and economic benefits as places where people can come to find out about local history and ways of life.

The three Welsh restoration candidates are all examples of buildings that were once common in Wales, but are now much rarer. As such buildings disappear it becomes all the more desirable to preserve at least some of those that remain. And it becomes desirable too that these buildings, no longer commonplace, are explained and interpreted. That way locals and visitors alike can understand their history – how and why they were built, how they were used, why they fell into disrepair and how they were given a new lease of life. They all have interesting and inspiring stories and to know them is inspiring in a new way: encouraging us to seek out yet more such ageing buildings to recycle and restore. ▪

Pembrey Court
Pembrey, Carmarthenshire

> "Set near a once-busy harbour, Pembrey was once a trading centre and the house was a valued landmark to ships sailing along this treacherous stretch of coast, the scene of many wrecks."

The houses of the upper classes had a huge importance in village and country life until the mid-20th century. From vast country mansions to smaller manor houses, they still have enormous glamour and the power to attract thousands of visitors who want to look at the best in art and interior decoration and to understand how the other half lived. But the significance of these houses goes much deeper than the glamour. First, they and their lands were the base for their rich owners as well as the host of people they employed, both household servants and farm workers on their estates. Second, they were power houses, the homes of people of influence – not just in the local area but also throughout the whole country.

So when a once-great house falls into ruin, when the fine paintings and furniture have disappeared and the glitter has gone, the building may still have fascinating historical stories to tell, stories that can come alive again when we examine the stones that are left. Pembrey Court is such a house, near the coast that looks out towards the beautiful Gower Peninsula to the west of Swansea.

Pembrey Court today is in a sorry state. Most of the roofs have gone leaving a shell of ivy-clad walls. Dominic Conway, a leading member of the Friends group that looks after the site recalls: 'I have worked in Pembrey for 17 years and during this time I have watched the ivy cover the walls. It was always there, but now it is rampant.' It is a sad end for a house with a history that stretches back to the 14th century.

In the Middle Ages the English kings had a continuous struggle to rule Wales. One architectural legacy of this struggle is the great castles of North Wales, built by Edward I to

subdue the country. There were smaller, still older, castles, too, like the one at Kidwelly not far from Pembrey. But English domination was not only achieved through castles. Many Welsh manors, including Pembrey itself, were held by Norman or English lords to ensure that English influence spread throughout the principality.

In fact the histories of Kidwelly Castle and Pembrey Court are closely linked. In the 12th century Kidwelly Castle was held by a powerful lord called Maurice de Londres and around 1128 he granted the manor of Pembrey to a member of the le Boteler or Butler family. The de Londres and Butler families were tied together by the feudal system, which governed the entire social hierarchy in the Middle Ages. Under this system the king owned all the land and granted some of it to his most prominent lords in return for support in times of war. These lords, or tenants-

Above A wooden window frame is inserted into this stone wall at Pembrey Court. The lintel at the top is a heavy timber, generously proportioned to take the weight of the masonry above.

Opposite Peeping through the encroaching ivy, the battlemented top of this building at Pembrey Court still looks both grand and medieval.

Above This interior, with its fallen roof timbers and invading vegetation, poses a big challenge to restorers, but while the walls are solid there is still hope for the structure.

Opposite The silhouettes of gable and chimney are masked by ivy and trees.

in-chief, might then grant parts of their landholding to sub-tenants, who in turn owed military assistance to the tenant-in-chief. So the Butlers of Pembrey had to provide five archers to Maurice de Londres and this group of fighting men would make up a small part of the force that de Londres had to supply to the king.

The feudal system continued to operate until shortly before the time when Pembrey passed into the Vaughan family, when an heiress to the estate married Sir Richard Vaughan, High Sheriff of Herefordshire, in 1530. It was the 16th-century Vaughans who extended the estate and rebuilt Pembrey Court to create the buildings that are visible today – essentially a Tudor house built around the remains of the Butlers' 14th-century home.

The Vaughans were people of substance. They held local office – later Vaughans were High

Sheriffs of Carmarthenshire – and Richard's son Sir Walter was also a Member of Parliament for his county. So although the system of feudal power and obligations had disappeared, Pembrey was still a place of power and influence. The house was not vast, but it was a substantial stone manor house. It had lots of chimneys, showing that its owners could afford to heat almost every room, and sizeable mullioned windows, again suggesting wealth since glass was not cheap and rooms with big windows also needed extra heating. The outbuildings included a solid stone barn that was given a touch of grandeur with the kind of battlemented parapet that is normally seen on a castle.

The Vaughans did well, but in the following century they backed the wrong side in the Civil War. As an ardent royalist, Sir George Vaughan was thrown into prison in Southwark and fined

£2,609 for 'delinquency' – in other words, for supporting the king. He must have recovered though, because by 1648 he was entertaining Oliver Cromwell during one of the parliamentarian leader's visits to Wales. But, like the Butlers before them, the Vaughans disappeared from Pembrey when the house passed again through the female line, this time into the Ashburnham family of Sussex.

The Ashburnhams, who had much property in England, never lived at Pembrey and the Court became home to estate stewards, water bailiffs and tenant farmers. But it was still a substantial house and when John Ashburnham visited in 1677 he reported: 'I saw Pembrey House, an old stone house, large enough and kept in good repair.' The thick stone walls, roofed with natural stone tiles, must have seemed good for a few more hundred years.

The tenants of the 18th and 19th centuries seem to have kept the place in good repair too. There was a restoration in the 18th century and in the 19th the great hall was divided horizontally in two, to provide extra rooms when the house became the residence of several families. It was probably at this time that the stone tiles of the roof were replaced with slates. The Ashburnhams sold the Pembrey estate in 1922 and the house was bought by the Bonnell family, who farmed there. But they left the house in 1970 – although they continued to farm the land – and the building remained empty. It has been slowly deteriorating ever since.

The stone rubble walls of the house, barn and cowshed have survived and the place is still full of fascinating original features – arches, chimneys, windows, fireplaces and so on. The roofs have virtually gone, although there is enough evidence left to restore them, and the floors have gone in some places, including the barn. In addition, practically the whole structure is covered in ivy. But there are some other tantalising fragments of evidence. One ornate wooden beam, one of the few surviving roof timbers in the house, is medieval, and so points to parts of the structure that survive from before the time of the Vaughan family. And old photographs show at least one finely panelled room.

Because of the all-pervasive decay – and the alterations to the building that have been made over the years – the whole site of Pembrey Court looks rather haphazard, with gables of varying

Village Voice

"Although the building looks in a bad state, we were hugely relieved to learn, when we consulted the experts, that it is restorable. Even tiny fragments can provide important clues – it is exciting to learn that things like a piece of carved stone can offer evidence about the history or structure of the building. Now lots of people are realising this and our dynamic core group of supporters is expanding."

JANICE PLANITZER Pembrey

heights, windows at different levels and extensions projecting here and there. It is the archetypal 'romantic ruin'. But with effort and funding, it could become so much more than this.

Reroofed and restored, the court could have any one of a number of uses – or perhaps play a combination of roles. Elizabethan houses are rare in Wales so one potential use is as an interpretative centre for Tudor history that could host visits of school children who are studying the period as part of the National Curriculum. There is a populous catchment area stretching from Swansea in the east to Carmarthen in the west and no doubt adult visitors would be interested too. Another idea is to use some of the rooms as office space for local community groups as well as providing an organic café and shop selling local produce. An educational exchange centre is a third possibility that has been discussed. The most likely outcome is a mixed-use scheme, combining benefits for both locals and visitors.

Any of these schemes would bring benefit to Pembrey. The village is a small community, but there has always been support for plans to save

the house. Dominic Conway says: 'In the 1980s the court was threatened with demolition and one man, John Evans, threatened to go on hunger strike if the demolition work was begun. The house was saved but various schemes to restore it have foundered.'

Pembrey has seen many changes in the past. Set near a once-busy harbour, it was once a trading centre and the house was a valued landmark to ships sailing along this treacherous stretch of coast, which has been the scene of many wrecks. Coal was extracted from beneath the sea in the 18th century, ironworking and copper-working began locally in the 19th, and a power station provided employment in the 20th until it closed in the 1990s. Now a country park, set against the backdrops of the Gower Peninsula and Carmarthen Bay, attracts visitors to the area and others come to sail, watch the wildlife or to walk. A restored Pembrey Court has a lot of potential to complement these activities. The house could provide employment and lift the spirits of all those who would like this evocative old house to be more than the picturesque ruin it has become. ■

Opposite The glass is gone and the sashes are badly broken, but this window is still repairable.

Below left Amongst the saplings, various fragments of old timber can give restorers clues about how the building was put together.

Below right Bare walls reveal more about the development of the building, including the positions of fireplaces, windows, alcoves and other openings.

Pen Yr Orsedd Quarry
Nantlle, Caernarfon

The slate industry was once one of the most important in Wales. It started on a small scale hundreds of years ago, when people realised that the rock, which splits easily into thin sheets, was an ideal roofing material – waterproof, light and widely available. So in many places in northern and central Wales, not to mention on the Lleyn Peninsula and Anglesey, small local quarries were started where people took the rock from near the surface, and slate

became the typical traditional roofing material across much of Wales.

In the 19th century this small local industry was transformed into a big business with international markets. At the beginning of the century the population of Britain was rising and the industrial cities were starting to grow fast. At the same time transport links were improving, with the development of the canals soon to be followed by the railway network. So when hundreds of thousands of houses were needed for the expanding industrial workforce, slate from Wales was the obvious roofing material. The biggest reserves were in north Wales and soon large, industrial-scale quarries were being developed here as miners dug deeper to supply the growing demands from cities such as Manchester, Birmingham and ever-expanding London. Welsh slate was even exported across the Atlantic.

So there was a boom for the North Wales slate industry, but at a cost. Conditions in the mines were appalling and dangerous. Unlike the small local mines, many of the large-scale operations were deep pits, so roof falls added to the dangers posed by unguarded machinery and the perils of lung disease. There were no health and safety laws, and work in many slate mines was more

"The mine was an entire community and one on which the wider community of Nantlle depended for its livelihood."

dangerous even than that at the coal face. And when the shift ended, most miners went home to squalid barracks or lodging houses. It was tough, but for most it was the only work on offer.

Once there was plenty of slate available, people discovered a host of other uses for it. Its heatproof qualities and its resistance to acid were valued by scientists, who found it ideal for laboratory benches. Its supreme flatness was prized by the makers of snooker and billiard tables too. Children learned their letters on writing slates. And all sorts of items, from gravestones to house decorations, steps to water

tanks, were made of slate. Slate mining rapidly became as important to north Wales as coal mining was in the south.

Nantlle, six miles or so south of Caernarfon, is in this slate-producing area and it was here that the Pen Yr Orsedd Quarry was established. Slate extraction on a large scale began around 1816 when the mine was owned by William Turner, an Englishman from the Lake District. But the mine really began to expand and flourish after it was bought by W A Darbishire and Co in 1863.

The Darbishires, who came from Ashton under Lyme and also had railway interests, were a

Above The landscape is one of contrasts, with heaps of spoil leading the eye towards greener fields.

Opposite A gate leads into a compact courtyard between three buildings. With no ornament to speak of, the architecture is all about utility.

Village Voice

"Once upon a time this industry employed thousands of people in this part of north Wales – this quarry alone once had 650 workers. Whole villages like Nantlle were built on the slate industry and so the quarry was at the heart of the community. If we could restore these buildings and create a skill centre here the place would once again be able to make a huge impact on the local economy. "

LES JONES Nantlle

dynamic family of business people with a belief in the benefits of technology. They quickly developed the quarry machinery, bringing in steam power and building new workshops. The expansion of the mine meant that by the 1890s, when extra buildings, including the mine offices, were put up on the site, there were around 450 men working at Pen Yr Orsedd.

The feverish activity that slate mining entailed involved back-breaking work by the large labour force. This was a deep pit, so slate was mined underground, and the nature of the work meant that far more waste rock than usable slate was extracted. The result was large spoil heaps, the dominant feature of any slate mine. At Pen Yr Orsedd they are framed by the stunning background of Snowdonia's mountains and the rather more mundane foreground of the quarry's buildings – winding houses, a barracks for workers, a hospital, a compressor house, slate mills and the workshops and offices that are the current restoration candidates.

The sheer number and scale of these structures points to the size of the operation and its impact on the local area: it was big business. Work continued until 1997, but by then the industry had been in decline for decades. Increasing competition from tiles – especially those cheaply made from concrete – reduced the demand for roofing slates, while two world wars reduced the manpower. One by one, the Welsh quarries closed.

Now Nantlle is a poor area, in which most people work for low wages in the public sector or nearby factories. There is little private enterprise and the village has no shops or post office. The decline has left the quarry buildings in disrepair. David Gwyn summarises the problem: 'The quarry buildings are getting worse. Slates are going in places and quite a lot of the corrugated iron has gone, so there is a steadily increasing risk, both from the elements and from vandalism.'

The elder of the two buildings for proposed restoration is the quarry office block. This is a single-storey T-plan building, built in two phases during the quarry's two periods of development – in about 1863, when the Darbishires took over, and between 1899 and 1907. The block is, appropriately enough, built of slate rubble with slate roofs. Both wings have sash windows and the later part of the building has a pair of doors

on opposite walls, through which the workforce came and went when collecting their wages.

Not far away is the other main complex of buildings, the workshops where the tools and equipment used in the quarry were mended and maintained. This structure was originally built in about 1900 as a steel-framed building with corrugated-iron cladding but was later covered in blocks of sawn slate. At right angles to this block is a set of three parallel extensions, each of slate blocks with slate roofs. Probably constructed on the site of earlier buildings and dating to the 1930s, they contained the quarry's smithy, woodworking shop and stores.

These grey buildings with brick chimneys look imposing enough from the outside, but further fascination lies within. The contents include some of the original smithy equipment,

storage racks, an overhead gantry crane, two railway lines and a small locomotive turntable. It is an impressive collection that straight away takes the visitor back to the working lives of the men who built and maintained the quarrying equipment some 70 years ago.

Buildings like this are an apt reminder that, important as the work of the quarryman was, there was much more to the working life of a large quarry than simply the extraction of the slate. There was machinery to make and mend, orders to process and wages to pay. And all this activity, separate from the mine but dependent on it, employed many people whose jobs were lost along with those of the miners themselves. The mine was an entire community and one on which the wider community of Nantlle depended for its livelihood.

Above A selection of interiors at Pen Yr Orsedd Quarry shows the range of finishes, from cosy plaster, through slate, to corrugated iron. A variety of machinery also remains.

Opposite Enormous wedge-shaped buttresses prop up one wall – there was no shortage of building stone here.

Opposite Long, slab-like pieces of slate make up the walls here, their colour complementing the green of the hills beyond.

Below Sheets of corrugated iron lie around the tiny turntable that was once used for the small locomotives that hauled slate around the site.

These buildings offer a huge opportunity. Repaired and reroofed, they could start a new working life. Rather than producing items for the mine, the custodians of Pen Yr Orsedd plan that they should become a centre for the production of heritage engineering items. The range of objects produced could extend from street furniture to Victorian-style conservatories, for which there is a clear demand and which could bring in an income. More ambitiously, the workshops could also produce more unusual one-off items, such as parts for historic buses or railway locomotives.

A venture like this, complementing rather than competing with the kind of engineering facilities that already exist, could be hugely beneficial to Nantlle and the local area. For a start, it would bring new jobs to an area of high unemployment. In addition, it would bring training – especially in traditional skills such as blacksmithing and carpentry, but also in allied business skills and marketing, and in high-tech areas such as computer-aided design. So the scheme could benefit the community for generations. David Gwyn puts it like this: 'I'm reminded of something an Estonian friend said

to me: "Give the poor man a fishing rod not a fish". The training and education could lead from an apprenticeship, to further education, to work.' It is a huge opportunity.

There is wide enthusiasm for the plans and the University of Wales, Bangor, has already expressed moral support and interest in integrating the scheme into its existing training and degree programmes in its School of Business and Regional Development. And there is plenty of support even closer at hand. One group, the local silver band, even turned down funding so that Pen Yr Orsedd might benefit from the money instead.

There is sometimes a tendency to see our industrial remains as sad reminders of lost glory. They hark back, after all, to a time when Welsh coal and slate mines were at the heart of the industrial revolution. The work and prosperity that they brought can seem lost for ever while the future seems to be in computer skills and service industries. But a restoration scheme like the one proposed for the quarry buildings could resolve this conflict between old and new. Combining the craft skills of the past with the technology of the present could lead to a vibrant future for Pen Yr Orsedd. ∎

Prichard Jones Institute
Newborough, Anglesey

> "What Sir John Prichard Jones gave Newborough was in effect a community centre. It was one of the most valuable gifts a village could have."

The story of Britain's buildings is full of monuments to the rich and privileged – big country houses are the best-known and most glamorous examples. But the rich did not always build purely for their own benefit. There are also hundreds of smaller buildings – rows of almshouses, schools, village halls, hospitals and so on – built by the rich for the benefit of those who were less well off. When a prominent local citizen decided to provide a building for his home town or village the result could be a landmark, a social asset, an educational resource or a combination of all

three. When Sir John Prichard Jones, successful department-store owner, decided to provide a building for his home village of Newborough on the island of Anglesey, it was just such an architectural hat-trick.

Sir John certainly had the money for such a gesture. He was one of the owners of Dickins and Jones, a well-established firm that had begun in the late 18th century as the mercers Dickins and Smith. In the 1880s, by which time the Welsh Jones family had entered the business, retailing was changing fast and the latest fashion was the department store, which had everything under one roof. The owners of Dickins and Jones saw the chance to expand and their Regent Street premises soon became one of London's premier department stores. It was a prosperous business, with commissionaires at every door to receive the well-heeled as they arrived in their carriages and cabs. In the 1890s they expanded further, buying up the stock of then well-known firms such as prominent silk mercers Lewis and Allenby and the Bond Street couturier Redmayne.

During this period of expansion the store was still run by members of the original families. There were two Dickins family members on the board and Sir John Prichard Jones was managing

Village Voice

"When you mention to people who have been brought up in Newborough that the institute might have to close they look at you in horror and say, 'It can't close!' This building has been at the heart of the community and the local people are to be commended for looking after it for so long. But now it's one hundred years old and it is only to be expected that it needs help."

GWYNNE JONES Newborough

director. Sir John was a committed philanthropist who provided the money for the large Prichard Jones Hall for the University of Bangor. Since his boyhood he had had the ambition to make his fortune and use some of the money to help his home village. An institute in the village of Newborough, plus six pensioners' cottages, 'for the benefit of the inhabitants of Newborough alone' was his gift.

Today the term 'institute' sounds remote and almost academic, but in Wales in 1905 it was forward-looking. What Sir John gave Newborough was in effect a community centre – one of the most valuable gifts a village could have. In those days only the very rich had a car, there was little public transport and most working people had neither the time nor the money to go far for their entertainment. For most it was the local pub or nothing. But pubs in the Edwardian period were for adults only. Most villages had nowhere for family entertainment; often there was not even a village hall where the people could gather on special occasions.

The notion of an institute was the particularly Welsh response to this problem. The idea was for a place with a 200-seat public hall where the community could gather for special events. In addition the building was provided with a coffee room where all the family could go and where there would be non-alcoholic drinks on sale so that people did not go there to get drunk. There was also a smoking room – in 1905 a room for the men of the village – and a corresponding 'ladies' room'.

And, most importantly, there was a library. Sir John and the other people who founded institutes in this period were keen that working people should be able to 'improve' themselves. Enid Mummery, secretary and treasurer of the trust that looks after the institute, explains Prichard Jones's motives: 'Above all he was interested in education, especially education for the poor. He was eager for people to have access to books and returned regularly to Newborough to see that the institute was being administered properly. After his death in 1917 his wife came for a number of years.'

Books and even newspapers were beyond the budget of most ordinary people. Here anyone could come and read, catch up on the news and come away better informed about the world beyond Anglesey. Prichard Jones's mission to educate people went further than the books

though. He saw to it that the walls were decorated with reproductions of paintings by well-known artists including J M W Turner. The masses had as much right to look at good works of art as the upper classes.

The style chosen for the institute was a kind of hybrid Tudor Revival style known to the Victorians and Edwardians as 'Old English'. It was a style that had evolved in the 1880s when prominent architects such as R Norman Shaw

were building large country houses for rich clients who wanted something different from, and less formal than, either the severe Classical-style buildings or the church-like Gothic houses that many Victorian architects were producing. Old English buildings were, by contrast, informal and asymmetrical. Soon the style was being used not only for houses, but also for shops, pubs and some public buildings. These structures used a mixture of materials, in particular combining

Above Beautiful details abound inside the institute: Art Nouveau door handles, stained glass and decorative tiling, and a finely crafted staircase.

Opposite The building sits near valuable green space in the village.

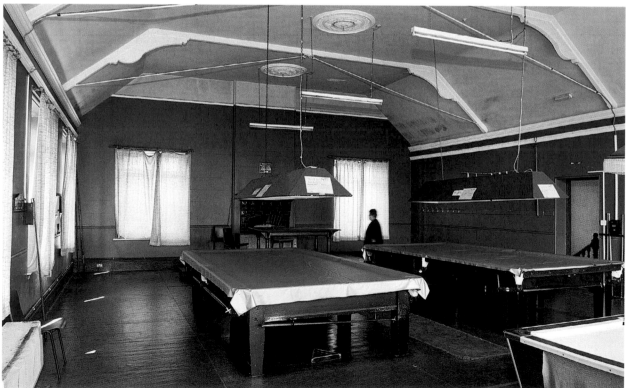

half-timbering with brick and stone. Big gables, recessed porches and the occasional tower were all typical features.

This is exactly what the people of Newborough got for their institute. Two big, half-timbered gables look out from the entrance front, with an off-centre, fancy-roofed clock tower between. Tall chimneys are another feature that recalls the Tudor buildings of the 16th century. Big windows let in lots of light and the contrast between the black-and-white upper floors and the stonework below catches the eye. It is an Old English building but, mindful that the Tudors originally came from Wales, the people of Newborough might have called it 'Old Welsh'. It looks impressive, and the neighbouring pensioners' cottages in the same style complement it well. Prichard Jones's gift certainly gave the village a focus and a bold identity all its own.

More than this, the building was designed to be used and it has remained popular as a local meeting place for more than 100 years. The large upstairs room is now a three-table snooker room, two of the downstairs rooms are still used for meetings of local groups and by agencies such as the Forestry Commission, and the historic library houses documents and books relating to Prichard Jones's mission to educate and enlighten people. It is a well-loved building and it has been well used.

As Enid Mummery points out, Prichard Jones was keen that the institute should last: 'Sir John Prichard Jones funded the upkeep of the institute by allocating the income from some of his London property to fund it. But when the Second World War came things changed. Many of his properties were bombed and the leases ran out. So the hall was left with a much smaller income.' The people of Newborough have kept it going with income from hiring rooms for events and the revenue from the local council, who now run the library and pay rent for the space. But it is not easy to do all the necessary maintenance on this small income.

Now, at just over 100 years old, the building is badly in need of repair. There is a pervasive damp and mould problem, in part at least because the roof is now showing its age. Repair of part of the roof would slow the deterioration, but experts estimate that it will need to be completely renewed within the next few years. There are

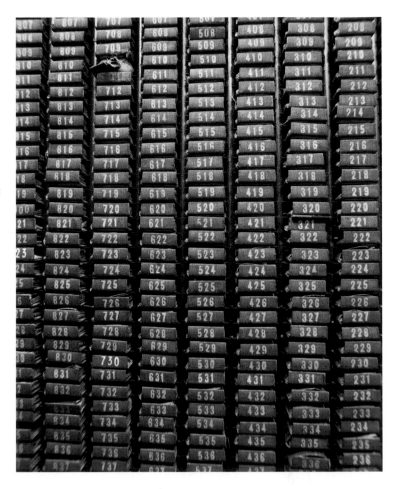

also signs of woodworm amongst the roof timbers. As well as these structural problems the building needs bringing into line with modern requirements. A new kitchen and proper disabled access, including a lift, are top of the list of necessary upgrades, so there is plenty to do.

The upside is that many of the building's original features remain, including fireplaces, wooden panelling, library furniture and stained glass, so there is huge potential for the building to shine once again. Once a restoration is completed the institute will continue to flourish as a focus for the Newborough community. Groups will queue up to meet here, there is potential for displays explaining the history of the medieval Welsh princes' court that met in Newborough, and there is also potential to let some of the rooms as office space to generate income to fund future maintenance. The Prichard Jones Institute will be good for one more century at least. ■

Above The original system of library record-keeping remains intact.

Opposite above The library is furnished with outstanding woodwork – there is no doubt that education was supremely important to Prichard Jones.

Opposite below This large room, with its snooker tables, could be turned into a generous assembly or meeting space.

Pembrey Court

Pen Yr Orsedd Quarry

EAST CHURCH
Cromarty, Highlands

Scotland

Scotland is well known as one of the most beautiful parts of the United Kingdom and it is also one of the largest regions, covering some 30,000 thinly populated square miles (78,000 sq km). Everyone has a picture in their mind's eye of Scotland, and it is likely to be one that includes mountains, forests and lochs. This is the dominant scenery of the Scottish highlands, the enormous region that makes up the northern portion of Scotland's mainland. Here, towns are few and far between and even villages are sparse. Visitors come for the scenery, for the sense of peace and quiet, and because this is the region where the most famous icons of Scottish culture, from tartan to whisky, originate.

To the south of this area are the central lowlands, where much of Scotland's population is concentrated in the great cities of Edinburgh and Glasgow – and in other centres such as Dundee. Still further south are the southern uplands, which stretch down towards the border with England. Here there are hills covered with great tracts of moorland but there is plenty of rich farmland too, especially in the Borders – an area with a history dominated by relations with England. It boasts many castles, built when people had to defend themselves from continuous cross-border raiding. It is also an area of ruined abbeys and notable small towns and villages.

Around Scotland's 2,300 miles (3,701km) or so of rugged coastline are the 790 islands that

DENNIS HEAD OLD BEACON
North Ronaldsay, Orkney

GREENLAW TOWN HALL
Greenlaw, Berwickshire

Left to right A neatly painted number on the seating at the East Church, Cromarty; the massive stone blocks at the entrance to the Old Beacon, Dennis Head; crisp Classical decoration at Greenlaw Town Hall – these details sum up the very different textures of the three Scottish restoration candidates.

make up the fourth element of the country. Like the rest of Scotland they are incredibly diverse, from the mainland's close neighbours such as Skye and Mull to the more remote Western Isles with their peat bogs and sandy beaches. Still more distant are the northern archipelagos of Orkney and Shetland – windy, remote and beautiful.

This quality of isolation is something that can dominate life in Scotland's rural communities. In the Highlands in particular, distances from one settlement to the next can be large, especially when you have to go halfway around a mountain or a loch to get from one place to another. This makes facilities such as local shops, schools and community centres still more vital. And the sense of isolation in the islands can be still greater.

The islands are good places to appreciate the sheer age of Scottish culture. Orkney is famous for its prehistoric monuments, which include the Stone Age settlement of Skara Brae, still virtually complete and, at well over 4,500 years old, a strong candidate for the title of Britain's oldest village. The standing stones of Lewis and Harris and the great Iron Age tower of Mousa Broch on Shetland are other notable monuments of prehistoric Scotland.

These ancient sites begin a tradition that is strong throughout Scotland, which boasts some 650 conservation areas and a fascinating portfolio of historic buildings, from baronial country houses to great industrial monuments. Scotland's historic rural buildings take their place beside these more famous sites. Rows of fishermen's houses in coastal villages, mostly harled (rendered) to protect them from the wind and weather, are a vital part of the rural scene. In the bigger settlements they also have slightly larger neighbours – merchants' houses that are taller and grander, and sometimes have an arcaded lower floor where business was transacted. There are notable religious and public buildings too, from churches to town halls, each of which has played a key role in their community and its history. And then there are the isolated farmhouses and crofts that drove the Scottish economy for centuries and are still vital in a region that produces some of our best beef and mutton.

Farming is still at the heart of rural life in Scotland and other traditional businesses, such as whisky distilling, continue to earn their keep in many areas. But in other ways Scotland is changing. New businesses such as telecommunications and the service industries are growing. Scotland has a world-class biotechnology sector and an expanding electronic industry. And tourism is still on the increase and promises to continue to be a major earner, with visitors drawn equally to Edinburgh's culture and nightlife and to the quieter attractions of the highlands. The future

seems to lie in these new industries or in the creative businesses that are also springing up, and they are drawing many of Scotland's young people away from a traditional rural way of life, and away from the village and agricultural heritage that has been left behind. It is a pattern that is familiar in many parts of Britain but is especially strong in Scotland where rural communities are so isolated.

This is an effect that is seen in all three of Scotland's restoration candidates. It takes its most extreme form on the Orkney island of North Ronaldsay, where the population is tiny and there are only a handful of children at the local school. Here, the restoration of the Old Beacon, the original 18th-century lighthouse at Dennis Head, promises to bring more tourists and income to the island and to create more employment. It is a good example of a restoration project that fits into a wider scheme, with a tourist trail that links it to other monuments on the island.

The church is another part of life which does not always attract the interest or commitment of the young. But the East Church at Cromarty, the restoration candidate from the Highlands region, has been at the heart of village life at least since the 17th century and probably for far longer. The solution here is for a restoration scheme involving hands-on involvement. It is hoped that the presence of a host of experts on the site, from masons to archaeologists, will encourage young

and old alike to acquire new knowledge and skills that relate directly to Scotland's history.

At Greenlaw in the Borders region it is a similar story. The old Town Hall is a building that speaks volumes about local history but has struggled to secure a lasting role. Its supporters, who have campaigned and planned for years for the building, hope that restoration will produce a beautiful building of which their whole community can be proud.

In their different ways, all these buildings bring to life key moments in Scottish history. The East Church at Cromarty is one of the best examples of the kind of place of worship that developed as a result of the Reformation, the moment when the church in Scotland turned its back on the traditions of Catholicism and developed the Bible-based, locally governed religious culture that still exists today. The lighthouse at Dennis Head was one of the first in a series of lights that protects shipping around Scotland's hazardous coasts and was built as the Northern Lighthouse Board, which still looks after Scotland's lights, was being formed. And Greenlaw's Town Hall is a superb example of a style of Classical architecture that was developed in Scotland to symbolise local civic pride. Restoring buildings like these is a marvellous thing to be doing, because the process brings alive Scotland's past while illuminating a pathway of hope for the future. ▓

East Church
Cromarty, Highlands

Opposite A view past the 18th-century graves in the churchyard shows Cromarty's East Church, with its two large, round-headed windows.

In the 16th century winds of change swept through the Scottish church. The Scots began to turn their backs on Roman Catholicism and to look increasingly to Protestant ideas. This meant all kinds of changes. Protestants rejected the authority of the Pope and found their inspiration in the word of God as enshrined in the Bible. They rejected elaborate rituals and richly decorated churches, placing emphasis instead on preaching the word. And, under the influence of the French-born religious reformer John Calvin, they abandoned the hierarchy of priests and bishops, adopting a form of church organisation in which ministers or presbyters made decisions collectively in meetings called councils or presbyteries – in other words the church became a Presbyterian church.

All these developments, which reflected changes seen across Europe from Germany to England, added up to the religious revolution known as the Reformation, and they had huge implications for church architecture. Churches became less ornate and, instead of the high altar, the focus of every church became the pulpit. The aim of church-builders was to create interiors in which as many people as possible could sit within easy listening distance of the pulpit, so that they could hear the sermon.

The East Church at Cromarty is one of the best examples of a Scottish church of the Reformation period. John Hume, former Principal Inspector of Historic Buildings for Historic Scotland, has described it as 'unquestionably one of the finest 18th-century parish churches in Scotland, the epitome of the development of Presbyterian worship during that century'. It is set in a beautiful walled graveyard in the heart of Cromarty, an attractive place that was once a prosperous port, on the north-eastern tip of the Black Isle – the peninsula between the Beauly, Moray and Cromarty Firths. It is likely that the church was here before the Reformation, but it was altered substantially in the late 16th or early 17th century when the fire of the Reformation was still burning brightly.

The East Church is a typical traditional Scottish building, with walls covered with harling – the Scottish term for render – and roofs of slate. Its graveyard is full of carved tombstones that tell the story of the people of Cromarty from the

"East Church was at the religious and social heart of Cromarty, a place that grew up around its large, sheltered harbour, much used by fishing boats in the hemp and ironware trades."

Above Seating fills almost every available space in the church, and none of the seats is very far from the main focus of the interior – the pulpit.

Reformation onwards, including memorials to merchants who lived in the fine old houses still to be seen in the village. The monuments include a number of locally carved stones bearing the skull-and-cross-bones design – a motif that is less to do with the burial of ex-pirates and more to do with the wish to remind passers-by of the inevitability of death. Against this rather sombre background the church stands proud and plain, its main adornments a small bell turret at one end and two large, round-headed windows in the middle of the long wall.

In the early 1700s a series of alterations began to make space for larger congregations, and to give the church interior its very special character. The first such modification was the building of a gallery or loft, known as the Scholars' Loft, above the western end of the church. Then in 1739–41 a northern extension was added, also with its own gallery, the Poor Loft. This changed the plan of the church from an oblong to a T-shape and greatly increased the building's capacity. In this

new layout all the seats look towards the junction of the 'arms' of the T, where a large pulpit is placed. The pulpit is flanked by the church's two large windows which, glazed with clear glass, flood the interior with light. The final addition was the most elaborate of the galleries, the Cromartie Loft of 1756, which was built above the church's eastern arm.

The Poor Loft was furnished with wooden box pews, most of which date from the 18th and 19th centuries and which enabled parishioners to sit and listen to sermons in relative comfort – the sides of the pews reduce drafts – while not getting so comfortable that they were tempted to fall asleep. In the building's well-lit interior they could also see clearly to read their Bibles or hymn books.

The light also gives the interior some of its special character. Victoria Collison-Owen, director of the Scottish Redundant Churches Trust that looks after the building, speaks of the effect of this natural light: 'The East Church is a very atmospheric building. The windows still have a lot of their early glass. This is hand-made crown glass, which throws the light in different directions. The effect of the light coming through the big windows is beautiful and very atmospheric. And the windows have a lovely view on to the graveyard and the trees beyond. So the East Church is a wonderful place to come to sit quietly. Even people who are not religious find a deeply spiritual quality in the building.'

This light illuminates a plain interior, dominated by white walls and wooden pews and gallery fronts. But look a little closer and there is plenty to see. Some of the pews are made of reused timbers on which survive various interesting paintings and inscriptions, including coats of arms of a once-prominent family who left the area. Initials on the gallery front of the Poor Loft remember parishioners including members of the Harper, McCulloch and Miller families. And a fine hatchment – a painted coat of arms used at a funeral – acts as a memorial to George Ross of Pitkerrie and Cromarty, a lawyer, businessman, local landowner and agricultural improver who made a huge investment in Cromarty in the late 18th century.

The East Church is an eloquent reminder of a typically Scottish form of Christianity and an

Left Reused timbers reveal fascinating bits of painting, testimony to a long-gone generation of benefactors.

Below A welcoming open gate leads to the graveyard and church.

ornament to Cromarty, a historical village which has many other listed buildings. For some 400 years it was at the religious and social heart of Cromarty, a place that grew up around its large, sheltered harbour, much used in turn by fishing boats, vessels involved in the hemp and ironware trades, and ferries. Like the church, the settlement had heydays in the 18th and 19th centuries and there are still many Georgian houses and Victorian cottages. It is quieter now, although the port is still important for the manufacture and

Village Voice

"The East Church means so much to local people – partly because it's a beautiful old building, but also because many families here have links with the church going back generations, in some cases hundreds of years."

NORA WATSON Cromarty

Above A commemorative board records the services provided by the local lifeboat in the early part of the 20th century, a reminder of Cromarty's close proximity to the sea.

Above right Elegant narrow glazing bars make a pattern of lines and curves in the large, clear glass that lets in plenty of light.

maintenance of oil rigs. But it is best known as the region's best-preserved historic settlement and is rightly proud of its heritage.

Among Cromarty's most famous sons are Sir Thomas Urquhart – the 17th-century writer and translator of the French novelist Rabelais – and Hugh Miller, a stone mason and passionate fossil-collector who taught himself about geology and wrote at absorbing length about his discoveries. Miller is remembered for his books on these subjects, especially *Footprints of the Creator*, *Testimony of the Rocks* and *The Old Red Sandstone*.

Miller was also a devout Christian. His work as a stone mason took him several times to the churchyard where he carved tombstones – the last he produced there was for his own daughter, Elizabeth, who died in infancy. But his most far-reaching religious gesture was a rejection of Cromarty's old church. Miller was a prominent

member of a movement for change in the Scottish church. An evangelical Christian, he believed that the existing church in Scotland was too much dominated by the landowners, who often tried to get their own candidates appointed to the ministry against the wishes of local parishioners. Miller backed the non-intrusionist cause and edited a paper, *The Witness*, which became the major mouthpiece for non-intrusionist views. There was a vigorous debate between the two sides which came to a head when the congregation at the East Church walked out one Sunday and a new Free Church of Scotland was born. Historians disagree about whether Miller himself was in the congregation that Sunday, but he wrote the event up in *The Witness* and ever since this key episode in Scottish history has been associated with the little East Church at Cromarty.

The unspoilt nature of the building and its interior, plus the role it played in the history of the church in Scotland, give the East Church a national importance. The building kept its importance for Cromarty too, through most of the 20th century. But in 1998 it was declared redundant and was handed over to the Scottish Redundant Churches Trust (SRCT).

Local people continue to care for the East Church and the building is still used for weddings, funerals and occasional services, notably those held during gatherings of the Urquhart clan, the descendants of the famous Sir Thomas. Concerts, exhibitions, a flower festival and a children's opera have all been held there. The church is kept open during daylight hours and some 8,000 people visit it every year. But, in spite of the efforts of devoted local carers and the SRCT, the building's condition is now giving cause for concern. Dry rot has been attacking it for years and although this has been partially treated there was not enough money to treat the entire structure, so it is still a threat. In addition, there is extensive damp and the roof is badly in need of repair. Add to this the activities of local vandals, and the risk to the church becomes clear.

But those who care for the East Church have not been idle. They have already obtained a project-planning grant from the Heritage Lottery Fund, which has enabled them to commission specialist surveys and work out what needs to be done. They are now seeking funds to restore the building before the damage gets worse, so that it can become an even greater asset to the community.

Their vision is very much one of a community building. The concerts, flower festivals and similar events will continue, but the plan is to go further than this and to engage the area's young people, especially those who are unemployed and could gain valuable skills in construction and conservation by getting involved in the project. While work is in progress, open days, 'hands-on' sessions, tours and presentations will keep everyone informed of what is being done and why. Victoria Collison-Owen stresses the importance of involving the local community: 'It is really important to us to involve local people in the project. Often conservation projects discourage people from getting involved, but we want to invite people in, to give them a hands-on involvement with the process of conserving a historic building. There is a huge opportunity for people to learn from all the experts who will work on the site.' The finished church will also contain information about the history of the building and educational facilities for school visits, so the message will be heard by the youngest members of the community.

The East Church has been central to Cromarty for centuries and its custodians want that to continue through the restoration project and beyond. They are hoping for a beautifully restored building, a time-capsule of the Scottish post-Reformation church that will be worthy of this historic settlement. More than this, they hope the restored church will both enthuse the people of Cromarty and bring in visitors from outside, reflecting once more both the local and national importance of this beautiful building. ▪

Below left A staggered row of neat wooden doors gives access to the seating.

Below right Initials carved into the front of one of the lofts commemorate members of prominent local 18th-century families.

Dennis Head Old Beacon

North Ronaldsay, Orkney

"So the sea is vital to the island, sometimes in unexpected ways, and the islanders have always been aware of the dangers associated with life on a treacherous coast."

Lighthouses are a way of life around our coasts and a matter of life and death. From the jagged Atlantic coast of western Ireland to the rough North Sea coast of eastern England and Scotland, they have been guiding shipping for centuries. By the mid-18th century some 40 lighthouses had been built around our coasts and more were added in the 19th century. Today the Northern Lighthouse Board runs and maintains 212 lighthouses around the coasts of Scotland and the Isle of Man.

Our most remote islands have always relied heavily on the sea for transport and none more so than the islands of Orkney, to the north-east of the Scottish mainland. These islands, mostly low-lying, windy and treeless, have beautiful landscapes of green grass, grey stone and blue sky. The environment is welcoming but for one major drawback – treacherous tidal currents, whirlpools and strong winds make the sea dangerous for shipping.

North Ronaldsay is around 30 miles from the Orkney mainland and is the most northerly of Orkney's inhabited islands. Boats approaching it have to cope with the treacherous waters of the North Ronaldsay Firth. This has kept the island isolated making shipping protection a priority.

William Muir, one of the islanders most closely involved with the lighthouse, describes how versatile you need to be to live on an isolated island like this one: 'North Ronaldsay is a small community, of around 70 people. When you live in a place like this you have to be able to do many different jobs, because some services are not available otherwise. I do some crofting and I work as a standby lighthouse keeper – although the light is automatic there has to be someone available on standby in case anything goes wrong. I also do some building work. Many who are crofters also do some fishing. So although we work on the land we are also very close to the sea and the lighthouse is a reminder of that.'

The people of North Ronaldsay have always relied on boats and the sea for travelling, trading and transporting essential supplies. And the sea has sometimes been a source of unexpected bounty. One valuable maritime resource was the abundant seaweed that washes up on the island's shores. Seaweed was used by the islanders as a fertiliser and as fuel, and from the 1720s onwards kelp-processing became an important industry here. Burning the seaweed in shallow stone pits produced an oily liquid that dried hard and was shipped south, where further processing extracted valuable minerals such as iodine.

Today these uses of seaweed have declined, but the material is still prized as an animal feed. Sheep-rearing is now among the island's most

Opposite Circular stone stells – enclosures for penning sheep – are a traditional part of the rural landscape at Dennis Head. The Old Beacon towers in the background.

Below Sheep are still a vital part of the economy here.

Above The Old Beacon stands proud in a landscape where water and pasture – not to mention old boats and sheep – come together.

Right The jetty is just as impressive a piece of engineering and stone masonry as the Old Beacon itself.

Opposite The cottage that nestles close to the foot of the Old Beacon is ruined now, but the lines of roofs and doorways can still be made out.

widespread activities. The farmers raise a traditional breed of sheep similar apparently to those farmed in prehistoric Orkney settlements such as Skara Brae. The business is especially profitable now, since restaurateurs as far away as London have recognised the fine flavour of Ronaldsay mutton, the meat made tender as a result of the animals' slow growth. By feeding their sheep on seaweed the farmers produce meat that is rich in omega oils too.

So the sea is vital to the island, sometimes in unexpected ways, and the islanders have always been aware of the dangers associated with life on a treacherous coast. These challenges became increasingly urgent during the 18th century, when trade between Europe's northern nations and the Far East was increasing. In 1740, for example, *Svecia*, a ship of the Swedish East India Company, set sail from Bengal on its way to Gothenburg. The vessel was an armed merchantman, well protected against attack with 28 guns. But guns offered no protection against the greatest dangers in the northern oceans – the weather and the currents. The ship was blown off-course, ending up in gale-force winds in the North Ronaldsay Firth, where she was battered against a line of rocks known as the Reefdyke.

After four terrible days on the rocks, *Svecia* went down. Some of those onboard escaped in a longboat to Fair Isle, some 27 miles (43km) east-northeast of North Ronaldsay. A few others went down clinging to an improvised raft of masts and rigging. Still others were washed up on North Ronaldsay with part of the ship's deck. The islanders, meanwhile, helped themselves to some of the vessel's rich cargo.

The sinking of *Svecia* was just one episode in a history of shipwrecks around the island. Only four years later another vessel, this time a Danish East Indiaman, was wrecked, although this time the crew and cargo were saved. It remained clear that something needed to be done to help those who had to travel through these difficult seas.

One of the first to do something was a hero of navigation, Murdock McKenzie. McKenzie, a Kirkwall man, began to plan a series of charts of the seas around Orkney in 1742. He raised money, acquired surveying equipment from the Admiralty and the East India Company, and by 1750 had published a series of accurate charts as *Orcades, or a Geographical and Hydrographical Survey of the Orkney and Lewis Islands*.

Village Voice

"We do have to find new ways of surviving. Crofting and fishing used to be the way of life here but farming's not what it used to be and now it's highly mechanised, and one farmer can do the work of probably 30 before, so we have to look at other ways of creating employment. The restoration project would create new tourist opportunities for the island and new jobs for this community."

WILLIAM MUIR North Ronaldsay

problem of navigation around Britain's northern waters. The commissioners were authorised by Parliament to build four lighthouses and in 1787 they appointed an Edinburgh lamp-maker and iron-smith, Thomas Smith, as their first engineer. Smith was trained and advised in lighthouse-building by another engineer, Ezekiel Walker of King's Lynn, and took on his stepson Robert Stevenson (ancestor of the famous writer Robert Louis Stevenson) as his associate.

By 1788 the laborious job of transporting materials from mainland Scotland had begun, and by the autumn of 1789 the stone tower, together with dwellings for the lighthouse keepers, was finished. It was an impressive structure, a stone tower some 70 ft (21m) in height containing a spiral staircase with stone treads cantilevered out from the walls.

The new light was first lit on 10 October 1789. The beam was produced by the latest in lighting technology, a catadioptric – or mirror-based – system, powered by a cluster of oil lamps below reflectors. Shining out from the most easterly point on Dennis Head it seemed to herald a new era of safe shipping around the island. But things did not go as smoothly as Smith and the people of North Ronaldsay had hoped. The wrecks continued – in part because seamen were attracted to the light, believing it to be a sign of safety.

So the dream combination of a good engineering team, a strong stone tower and the best in lighting had not worked. A new lighthouse at Start Point on the western end of the island of Sanday seemed to present a partial solution and this was completed in 1806. So, in 1809, the light at Dennis Head went out for the last time. The lamp was removed, a large stone ball, 8 ft (2.4m) in diameter, was placed at the top of the Dennis Head tower and the building was made definitively redundant.

But the story was still not over. Seamen and locals were still convinced that a light was needed at Dennis Head but in a different location, to give maximum warning of the treacherous Reefdyke. So in 1850 a new site was chosen and Robert Stevenson's son Alan was selected as engineer. Stevenson recommended a very tall tower, with all the extra cost that this entailed, and the structure finally built was 139 ft (43m) high. It was completed by the Leith builder William Kinghorn in 1854 and it remains the tallest land-

McKenzie's charts gave excellent guidance to sailors, but they could not prevent the area's treacherous weather from bringing more ships to grief. Between 1773 and 1788 alone there were 16 wrecks off the North Ronaldsay coast. A more radical solution was needed.

In 1786 a body called the Commissioners of Northern Lighthouses was formed to address the

based lighthouse in the British Isles. Now controlled automatically and provided with an upgraded light and radio beacon, it is still guiding shipping today.

This sequence of events has left behind it a fascinating heritage of buildings. First there is the Old Beacon, which has stood unused since 1809 after its 20-year working life, and its cousin the New Light. Then there are the keepers' cottages, built for the operators of the two lights, which are redundant in the age of automatic lighthouses. And there is another notable structure, the Bewan Pier: a stone jetty half a mile in length built by Kinghorn at the time the new light was constructed.

Now there are plans to restore these historic structures under a unified plan as part of the island's tourist industry. As William Muir explains: 'There is a history of tourism here – we always liked to take visitors up to see the light. But now it will be more formalised. The trust is licensed and insured to take people up and it's tremendous that when people visit the New Light they'll be able to see all the old equipment that is still there. Now we are creating a tourist trail with the Old Beacon included and facilities such as a tea room and a shop.'

The plan is for the Old Beacon to form the last stop in the tourist trail around the island – the buildings offer a perfect climax for a tour of the island. Displays about the history of lighthouses

and telling the story of the islanders' relationship with the sea could provide a focus. And it is hoped to restore the old lighthouse cottages so visitors can see what life was like in them 200 years ago. The entire scheme could bring in much-needed income from tourism – there is nothing else like it in Orkney.

To bring this vision to fruition will require a lot of work. The Old Beacon needs new windows, a new door and a thorough external repointing, and the staircase inside needs to be replaced. It is proposed to repair the masonry cap and to recreate the access balcony, as well as repairing the pier and restoring the cottages. As an interesting addition it is hoped to build a replica light at ground level, so that visitors can see how the Old Beacon worked when it was first built. A host of general facilities, from visitor toilets to floodlighting, waterworks to an access road, will also be needed.

It will be a long haul, especially for a small community like North Ronaldsay. But a multi-phase approach has already been drawn up to divide the work into manageable parts. If this is successful the island will have a new and lasting asset, a centre that provides education, information for visitors and a source of employment. Strengthening still further the connection between the island community and the sea will, it is hoped, also be a valuable investment into North Ronaldsay's future. ■

Above left Sash windows light the keepers' cottages next to the New Light. These buildings are not part of the restoration project, but are an important backdrop to the Old Beacon.

Above right The keepers' cottages by the New Light are single-storey, rendered structures.

Town Hall, Greenlaw
Greenlaw, Berwickshire

Opposite The wall beneath the dome at Greenlaw Town Hall has a series of openings surrounded by carved laurel wreaths, ancient Classical symbols of triumph and victory.

Below left The bust of Sir William Purves Hume Campbell commemorates the benefactor of Greenlaw Town Hall.

Below right Carved heraldic beasts still stand proud, if a little weathered.

With their old cottages, still older churches and a way of life that can follow the same pattern year after year, villages can seem timeless places. But life in the country is as subject to change as life anywhere else and the signs are often right there, in the buildings. Take the improbably grand Town Hall in the middle of the quiet Scottish village of Greenlaw. Its sophisticated design, with dome and Classical columns, would not be out of place in Edinburgh. But Greenlaw is in the Borders, a mainly rural region with few large towns. It is a quiet area for the most part, a place of small settlements and farms. The Town Hall at Greenlaw, by contrast, looks like an important urban building, and suggests that this place was once more prominent than it is now.

And so it proves. The name gives the game away, for Greenlaw Town Hall is also known as the County Buildings – Greenlaw was once the county town of Berwickshire. It had been raised to county-town status in 1698, because the original county town, Berwick on Tweed, had been in English hands since the late 15th century. The local Earls of Marchmont had pushed to make Greenlaw the county town and they built two of Greenlaw's most important structures, the gaol and the courthouse, in the early 18th century.

In 1828 the people of Greenlaw decided they needed to complete their set of civic buildings with a new town hall, but they could not decide how to pay for it. Local benefactor Sir William Purves Hume Campbell, a member of the Marchmont family, stepped in and construction

"The Town Hall at Greenlaw looks like an important urban building, and suggests that this place was once more prominent than it is now. And so it proves."

Village Voice

"The Town Hall is right in the centre of Greenlaw and it's a very powerful building. It was built to bring a sense of grandeur to the village and, if restored, it could do so once more. I think if it was restored people – even those who are daunted by the difficulties of restoring it – would get a tremendous buzz if they were able to walk through those pillars and use the building themselves."

MATTHEW GIBB Greenlaw

was soon under way. The foundation stone was laid on 4th August 1829 and the hall was completed at the end of 1831.

The people of Greenlaw must have realised that the building was going to be something special when the foundation stone was laid. There was a grand ceremony attended by a number of local dignitaries including the sheriff of the county, the parish minister, members of the court, a representative of the Marchmont estate and several prominent Freemasons. The minister offered a prayer for the success of the project and for 'long life and happiness' for Sir William. And Vice-Admiral Sir David Milne Home, who laid the foundation stone, made a speech referring to the stone as 'a sacred deposit in the charge of the inhabitants of Greenlaw'.

As a further indication of the historic importance of the event, the 19th-century equivalent of a time capsule was laid among the stones. This consisted of three bottles containing coins of the realm, contemporary newspapers and lists of the office-bearers of the Royal Arch Freemasons of Scotland. These bottles are still buried somewhere in the masonry, probably near the foundation stone at the north-eastern corner of the building.

The building that rose above the foundation stone cost £6,500, a considerable sum in the early 19th century, but Sir William's generosity was not all altruism. He knew that the hall would increase the town's prestige, giving it the edge over its local rival Duns, bringing more people into the locality and increasing his income from rents. So he would have wanted a building of quality and he got one so elegant that it probably seemed good value for his money.

This was largely due to the choice of architect. The Town Hall was designed by John Cunningham, a Berwickshire man who had studied architecture in Edinburgh and set up in practice there. In Edinburgh, Cunningham was exposed to the best in Classical architecture – the elegant buildings of the city's New Town that combined designs inspired by the ruins of Greece and Rome with the latest in town planning. His design for Greenlaw Town Hall had the same Classical elegance.

The requirement was for a large main hall flanked by smaller rooms, and Cunningham's design expresses this with a central block topped by a dome with smaller pavilions on either side. The central entrance has a pair of tall columns carved with Ionic capitals – the ancient Greek design made up of paired spirals. Other Classical details, such as triangular pediments, adorn the side pavilions making a symmetrical design that still looks stunning on the village square. The beautiful dome, standing on a stone 'drum' with round windows, each surrounded by a carved laurel wreath, makes a fitting climax to the structure. No wonder the people were pleased with the hall, and installed a marble bust of Sir William in the vestibule as a token of their gratitude.

This was a practical building too, with a 6oft-long (18m) hall for meetings and court sessions – and for Masonic rituals, for the members of the craft clearly had a large stake in the Town Hall. In the dome was a fire-proof room where local records were kept. This room turned out to pose a problem, however, because after it had been used for a few years as a record-store it was discovered that damp was getting in, and the records had to be moved to a room in the east wing.

Opposite below The layout of the Town Hall consists of a tall central portion with a pair of low side wings – a similar design to many grand country houses.

Opposite above This Corinthian capital is showing its age, but the elegance of its acanthus-leaf decoration can still be appreciated.

Below The decorative finishes have gone from the interior of the dome, a part of the building that has always suffered from damp.

Above left Some of the interior surfaces, like this door and catch, are damaged but repairable.

Above right Banded masonry awaits the attention of the restorer.

In spite of the damp dome, the hall was on the whole well built and made an attractive focal point for the town. It also turned out to be one of Cunningham's best Scottish buildings. A couple of years after the hall was finished the architect moved to America, but he failed to settle there and ended up in practice in Liverpool, where he designed some of the city's most prominent buildings, including the old Philharmonic Hall which, before it burned down in 1933, was considered one of the best concert halls in the world.

Greenlaw's much smaller hall served the community well until it ceased to be county town in 1903, losing its status to its old rival, Duns. Since losing its original role, the building has had several different uses. In the early 20th century it served Greenlaw as a village hall, before housing Polish prisoners of war during the Second World War. In 1973 it was converted for use as a swimming pool, but when a better pool was opened in Duns it lost this role too. Next it was reopened as a youth club and, more recently still, it was let to an antique dealer as a sale-room and store.

Time has taken its toll on the Town Hall. Local resident Susan McLean remembers realising that the building was in need of help: 'I have lived in Greenlaw for 25 years and my office overlooks the Town Hall, so I've watched it deteriorating for a long time. I can remember standing on the steps of the hotel opposite and seeing it set beautifully against a clear, star-lit sky, and thinking that something ought to be done to save it. So about 12 or 13 years ago a group of us – my late husband Sandy, Alistair Appleton, and I – decided to get an action group together to restore the building.'

They soon discovered that the building was in even poorer condition than it appeared. Although the main hall was reroofed in the 1940s, and more recently the interior of the building has been treated for wood rot, there are still problems with the roofs and rainwater has got inside in various places. Both rising damp and rainwater have damaged large areas of the walls, with the lower courses of stonework especially badly affected. A lot of the stone details are also badly weathered or damaged. Inside, there are further problems. Many of the interior finishes have been destroyed by damp and much interior decoration had to be removed anyway when the rot was being treated. Now it is unsafe even for small-scale public functions and the windows are boarded up. This at least protects the window frames, but also contributes to the damp, ill-ventilated atmosphere inside. Restoration will be a big job.

Although the building continues to deteriorate there is now some hope for its future. Over the last ten years or so various efforts have been made to save the building, with grant applications to major heritage bodies and various plans for new uses. There have been false starts, but they have taught people more about the building and about the ups and downs of applying for funding. Susan McLean stresses their determination: 'We are refusing to give up. We have good support from people such as Lady Bridget McEwen, our most long-standing trustee. And we are planning a mixed-use scheme for the building, part commercial and part community use, so that the building earns an income to fund its upkeep. We want it to be an inspiration for our community for years to come. I would like the restored building to be a fitting memorial to my late husband.'

So local people and planners are working together to find a future use for the building. It is clear that the cost will be high, because the damage to the building has not just caused the destruction of decorative finishes but affects key structural elements, and extends from the surface of the exterior stonework to the structure of the roof. But it is worth investing in a project like this, not least because the Town Hall has been a focus for Greenlaw for almost 200 years. Its strong Classical design by an Edinburgh-trained architect is typically Scottish and seems to symbolise the movement of this kind of high design from the metropolis to the countryside. And although it looks like a metropolitan building in a rural setting, it is in a way fitting that it should be here in the rural Borders. This has always been a region with a strong local identity and the Town Hall seems to embody this local spirit. It is also a building with enormous potential, with both a large meeting or exhibition space and smaller side rooms that could be put to a range of uses. It has survived various threats, from vandalism to the proposal in the 1970s to demolish it to make room for a car park. It richly deserves the new lease of life that restoration should bring. ▪

Top The incursion of damp has brought down ceilings in some rooms.

Above This room has fared much better and some decorative finishes survive.

Left Peeling paint is a call to action. Damage like this can be a symptom of deeper problems.

Old Beacon, Dennis Head

Greenlaw Town Hall

East Church, Cromarty

Northern Ireland

Northern Ireland is one of the most beautiful parts of the United Kingdom. Apart from the dense concentration of population in and around Belfast it is largely rural, with a series of stunning landscapes – coastal and inland, upland and lowland, natural and man-made. Parts of it feel as if they have not changed for centuries but, like any rural area, Northern Ireland has seen its fair share of change and gets much of its character from the dynamic processes of agriculture.

Around the coast, though, the scenery feels ancient. The north coast has a dramatic shoreline of rocks and caves, with the Giant's Causeway – the great rock formation of basalt columns in County Antrim – its most famous landmark.

The cliffs stretch for miles around the coasts of Antrim and Londonderry, while further west and south the great coastal loughs, such as the vast Strangford Lough, are havens for birds and marine wildlife of international importance.

Inland the scenery gives way to mountains and Northern Ireland's lush fields, home to the thousands of small farms that have provided a living for the region for centuries. These fields benefit from a climate that is notoriously wet, but also temperate. All grass-eating animals do well here, and the province has long been renowned for its dairy produce as well as for its beef cattle and sheep. This form of agriculture has left a clear mark on the countryside. Deep green fields, a cluster of low farm buildings, a network of

FORMER PARISH CHURCH
Cushendun, County Antrim

stone field walls – these are the elements that make up much of rural Northern Ireland and still provide the backdrop for the lives of a large proportion of its people.

Farming is still hugely important in Northern Ireland – although the numbers are declining, a bigger proportion of the population work on the land here than in any other British region. Though most of the farms are still small, a trend towards amalgamation is making some of them larger. Even so, few farms generate a sizeable income and many would not make a profit if they could not rely on income from other sources. Subsidies from the European Union are vital to most Northern Irish farmers, and many farmers or their spouses now have some other form of

income too. Good grass is an asset, but it is not necessarily a guarantee of riches.

Nevertheless, Northern Ireland has been an optimistic place since the peace process gathered momentum. Productivity and output are on the up and there are jobs to be found – indeed the region is recording its lowest unemployment rates ever. But few of these jobs are in the countryside and getting to work for many country people is likely to mean a commute to the nearest town or city. This trend is set to continue, because Northern Ireland has a surprisingly young population (with almost 60 per cent of residents currently under 40) and the rural population is generally more youthful than that in the towns.

Evocative details reveal something about the taste of previous users of Northern Ireland's restoration candidate buildings.
Above left A graffiti portrait in a carefully drawn frame on an interior wall at Gracehill Old Primary School.
Above right A ceramic bowl has been left on top of a stove at Cushendun church.

Opposite A pile of hymn books at Cushendun, some of which are stamped with the name of the nearby church of Layde.

So, as in virtually every rural area, access to facilities and employment is a huge issue. It is not only jobs that are most plentiful in the cities; facilities such as shops and post offices are often miles away from most farms and villages and virtually everyone needs a car to access key services. Ireland's roads are not as quiet as they once were.

Tourism is on the up too, so there are still more people moving around – to the benefit of the economy. Visitor numbers from all the main tourist markets have grown and there has been a marked increase in tourists from the all-important USA with its strong Irish links.

So the tensions between urban and rural areas, between progress and conservation, are as acute here as anywhere else. Although Northern Ireland has sometimes been criticised for neglecting its listed buildings, there have been some good initiatives. Since the province's first Conservation Area – Gracehill – was designated in 1975, another 58 have followed and they range in size and scope from large town centres to small residential areas, streets and villages. In 1998 the Townscape Heritage Initiative, focused on Conservation Areas, was launched by the Heritage Lottery Fund to work together with a whole range of partners, from companies to charities, to help conserve the built environment.

These days people realise that this push to protect old buildings need not conflict with the region's social and economic needs, and these two very different requirements come together in Northern Ireland's restoration candidate buildings. One, the 19th-century former parish church at Cushendun, is an ideal community space, a venue suitable for both classes and concerts that is already provoking a lot of interest among local groups.

It is a similar story with the Old Primary School at Gracehill, right in the heart of Northern Ireland's first Conservation Area. With the local children rehoused in a more modern school building there is a special chance to provide a community facility at the old school. There is also the challenge of conserving the building in a way that complements Gracehill's historic 18th-century Moravian village, a unique settlement that was planned along very specific lines. When they first built Gracehill, the Moravians deliberately planned the village around the social centre provided by the church and school. Their insistence on providing the communal buildings that the people needed is a lesson to us all as we look at the ways in which village structures need to be restored in the 21st century.

In their different ways, these restoration projects show the way forward for rural Northern Ireland. They both have a huge contribution to make to the life and economy of a small community. And each, in its own way, gives us pause for thought. ■

Old Primary School
Gracehill, County Antrim

"Life here was communal and cooperative. Most of the villagers were craftworkers…the revenue from their labours went into a central fund."

The Reformation – the great religious movement that led to the formation of the Protestant church – had various founders, but one of the most important was a man called Jan Hus (c. 1369–1415), a priest from Bohemia in what is now the Czech Republic. Hus preached a return to the basics of Christianity, for example supporting the use of local languages rather than Latin in church services and rejecting the corrupt practices of some Catholic priests. After Hus's death a number of his followers organised themselves into a separate church, known as the Bohemian Brethren.

Life was not easy for the Brethren. They were persecuted, especially during the Thirty Years War (1618–48), a political and religious conflict that devastated much of central Europe. After the war there were fewer and fewer places in central Europe where the Brethren could practise their religion openly. Many emigrated, but a few remained in Poland and in Moravia – the eastern portion of the Czech Republic.

In the 18th century a German nobleman called Nicolas Ludwig von Zinzendorf took pity on the Brethren, by now known as Moravians, and allowed a group of them to build a settlement on his lands in Saxony. Here they eventually thrived, and they became well known for their piety, their peaceful ways and their belief in education for all. Similar small settlements of Moravians were soon being formed at various sites in northern Europe and North America. One of the most famous was the town of Bethlehem in Pennsylvania. Another was the small settlement founded in 1765 near Ballymena in Northern Ireland – the village of Gracehill.

Today Gracehill is still a peaceful place. David Johnston, a local GP and member of the Gracehill Old School Trust, emphasises its tranquil atmosphere: 'In the often troubled history of Ireland Gracehill became known as an oasis of calm, and people have been commenting on the atmosphere of peace that pervades the place almost since the village was founded. Moravian communities from Ireland to South Africa have been at the forefront of reconciliation since the 18th century.'

You can detect this throughout the village. Visitors admire the well-landscaped graveyard and the village green, planted and cared for more like a garden than the grass plots that constitute many village greens in Britain. And the Moravians of Gracehill always maintained good relations with their non-Moravian neighbours. Although they were a missionary group who aimed to convert others, they did not make a

Opposite The restrained surround of the Old School's entrance with its Classical mouldings is just visible behind a pair of gate piers. The front windows have moulded surrounds, each with a protruding keystone at the top which has four facets, like a shallow pyramid.

Above A round-topped window with a pleasing arrangement of glazing bars in the end wall of the school.

Right The classrooms have 20th-century paint schemes.

Far right Earlier fittings such as ornate fireplaces reveal the school's long history.

Opposite With its pale façade, rows of windows and grey roof the Old Primary School is an imposing landmark in the centre of the village.

nuisance of themselves among the locals. They hoped more than anything to convert people by their good example in leading a peaceful and fruitful life in their beautiful village.

Built on land leased from Lord O'Neill, Gracehill was approached along an avenue of ash trees and centred on a green with a gravel path for relaxing walks. As well as rows of neat Georgian-style family houses, carefully arranged on a grid plan, there were communal houses accommodating single brothers and sisters, a farm, a shop and an inn. At Gracehill's heart were the church, the manse and the school. Not far away was the burial ground, the quietest place of all in this oasis of tranquillity, with women's graves on one side and men's on the other. All the gravestones lay flat on the ground, to avoid any implication of hierarchy that might come from one being taller than another.

The life lived here was communal and cooperative. Most of the villagers were craftworkers, with many lace-workers and weavers, and the revenue from their labours went into a central fund. The community gave each person a home and a living, using the rest of the money to maintain the village and fund the Moravians' missionary work.

Much of the architectural setting for this way of life remains today, from houses to church and graveyard. Fittingly, the village was declared Northern Ireland's first Conservation Area in 1975. At its heart is the school, one of the village's largest and most imposing buildings. Standing right in the middle of the village, its importance in both the life and the visual appeal of the place is clear.

Gracehill's Old Primary School was built in around 1780, some 15 years after the settlement's foundation in 1765. It served the community well, remaining in use as a school until 1999 when the pupils moved to a new building nearby. Since then it has stood empty and has grown increasingly dilapidated. Local residents soon become anxious at the state of the school and formed the Gracehill Old School Trust to acquire the building, conserve it and use it for the benefit of the community. The story since has been one of gradual fundraising and planning by the community of Gracehill to make best use of this valuable asset.

And an impressive asset it is. From the outside it is a typical Georgian building, beautifully in

Village Voice

"Gracehill is much visited, both because it is the only complete Moravian settlement in Ireland and because people find it such a special, peaceful place. The core of the village, where the school is, looks very much as it did in the early 19th century. But Gracehill is also a living community and the people of the area could benefit hugely if the Old School were restored."

DAVID JOHNSTON Gracehill

tune with the rest of this very special 18th-century village. Rows of windows look out across the entrance road and small windows peep out of the pitched roof, indicating apparently a building with two main floors and an attic.

This was indeed its original layout, but the building underwent major internal alterations during the 1920s to bring it more in line with the kind of school buildings that were fashionable at the time. Much of the first floor was taken out to create big classrooms with high ceilings. This change also restricted access to the large attic, which can now only be reached by ladder through a narrow access point. So the interior now consists of a high-ceilinged main floor, a vast and undulating attic and a long-unused basement.

Now the building is suffering from its years of neglect. There is damage from water penetration and wet rot, and there are also problems in the roof where a fire caused some damage a few years ago. As a result of this much of the attic floor is unsafe – but a great deal of the fabric is sound and the building, with its combination of large and small rooms, offers huge potential for community use. The profusion of windows makes the interior pleasant and light and outside, of course, the Old Primary School is still a gem in this village of visual delights.

The planned restoration will make the building look better still. The replacement UPVC window frames will be removed and wooden, Georgian-style sash windows will be installed. A row of new, sympathetically-styled rooflights will let more sun into the attic space.

The Gracehill Old School Trust has already made a lot of progress. In 2005 they obtained stage-one approval for a grant of just over £1,000,000 from the Heritage Lottery Fund. This means that the money will be held while the Trust continues with further necessary fundraising and works up more detailed plans. When restored the building is likely to include a visitor centre, café, community space and an after-school club – a blend of facilities that will serve the local population and visitors alike. David Johnston insists that there will be numerous benefits for the community: 'Exhibitions will keep people informed about the history of Gracehill; education projects and living history events will help local schools and complement the National Curriculum; the restored building will provide local facilities such as toilets and a tea room.'

Education was always most important to the Moravians. John Amos Comenius, the famous 17th-century bishop of the Moravian Brethren, was a pioneering scholar who wrote widely about both the theory and practice of education. So it is appropriate that education should be at the heart of the plans for the Old Primary School at Gracehill. David Johnston emphasises the project's importance: 'There is no doubt that the school is of local and regional importance, but its significance may go even wider. Gracehill is part of a network of Moravian villages that includes settlements in Denmark, South Africa and the USA. We have many plans for continued cooperation.' One of the results of this network is the Christiansfeld Initiative, named after a Moravian settlement in Denmark. The plan is to work together to get the settlements jointly nominated to UNESCO's list of World Heritage Sites. The restored school at Gracehill, central to this fascinating village, would be the perfect focal point for this omportant historic community. ■

Above The railings in front of the school were built with a series of downward-sweeping curves to allow for the sloping site.

Opposite top A steeply pitched roof and wide floor area allow for generous attic rooms.

Opposite bottom A rear view of the building shows the large windows in the end wall and the expanse of pale masonry at the back.

Former Parish Church
Cushendun, County Antrim

Opposite Cushenden's former parish church has a central nave, with a tower at the western end and a small vestry at the east.

Below The pointed-arched Gothic style in its plainest form is used for the details of the church, including this small doorway.

Location is key to the history and life of all villages. More often than not, if you understand why a village is sited where it is you can understand its history and development. At first sight the location of Cushendun – a picturesque village on the far north-eastern coast of County Antrim – seems remote and hard to comprehend. But if you look out to sea the site is easier to fathom. Cushendun is little more than 30km across the water from the Mull of Kintyre; it is the closest landing-place on Ireland's coast to the British mainland and there has been a harbour here since people first settled in this part of Ireland.

Even so, it is still a remote village with a sea connection to a still more remote part of Scotland.

As a result trade came through its port, but not on a huge scale. So fishing was probably just as important to the local way of life and salmon nets can still be seen there, testimony to the only local industry in this quiet corner of Antrim.

But in the 19th century one man had ambitions to make Cushendun a more important centre of trade. Local businessman Nicholas Cromelin hatched a plan to build a state-of-the-art harbour there, hoping to attract trade from Ballymena and other places in the surrounding area. In 1830 Cromelin hired the noted engineer Sir John Rennie to build the new harbour and was hopeful that the government would invest in the project. But, aware that some of Cromelin's other ventures had foundered, the government pulled out and the scheme came to nothing. Cushendun seemed fated to remain a backwater.

Around 80 years later there was another, more successful, development. In 1912 landowner Ronald John McNeill (later First Baron of Cushendun) commissioned the architect Clough Williams-Ellis to design a village square and seven houses. Williams-Ellis and another architect, Frederick MacManus, added more houses later. Williams-Ellis later became famous as the designer and developer of the Welsh village of Portmeirion, a fantasy village in the Italian style, and was known for the kind of inventiveness that produced filling stations shaped like Japanese pagodas. At Cushendun he was more restrained but equally inventive, creating cottages like those in Cornish fishing villages.

A Cornish fishing village on the Irish coast is a curious concept but it works, and today most of Cushendun is owned and cared for by the National Trust as a lasting tribute to the vision of both McNeill and Williams-Ellis. By McNeill's

"In centuries gone by the church was the centre of any village. It housed all sorts of functions, from local meetings and courts to schools and charitable works."

Village Voice

"Since we began seriously to explore ways of restoring the church the community has been galvanized, and there has been phenomenal enthusiasm and excitement about the project in the village. A restored church would become a much-needed focus for Cushendun. It would also help to draw in visitors and provide a centre for local groups and for events such as summer schools and exhibitions."

KATY ENGLISH Cushendun

time Cushendun already had its parish church, but an earlier McNeill had a hand in its building, at around the time of Cromelin's abortive plans for a new harbour.

In the early 1800s three local families, the McNeills, the Whites and the MacDonnells (the family of the Earl of Antrim), gave land on which a new church could be built because they sought a Protestant place of worship for their families and servants. The parish church of Cushendun was built on this land during the 1840s and the people of the village were buried in the graveyard surrounding it. It was, and still is, a compact, simple building seating around 80 people – quite big enough for the still-small village that surrounds it.

Like most 19th-century churches it was built in the Gothic style – an architectural style that was developed in the 13th century, lasted throughout the Middle Ages, and was revived in the Georgian and Victorian periods. Gothic style is characterised by pointed arches, tall interiors, pinnacles and towers. Perfect examples can be seen in our great cathedrals, where the church had money to spend on 'luxury' features such as stone-vaulted ceilings and enormous stained-glass windows. In smaller churches the style is usually more modest, but its features can still make a small building feel special, as they do at Cushendun.

The old parish church is built mainly of red sandstone and is in three parts: a central nave where the congregation sat, a tower and a small low structure at the eastern end used as a vestry. The nave is dominated by its windows, pointed at the top in the Gothic manner and divided by bars of stone in a simple Y-pattern. These tall, narrow windows emphasise the height of the small nave, making it seem grander and higher than it is. The tower is simple and elegant, with Gothic openings fitted with louvres to let out the peal of the bells, and pinnacles pointing skywards. The small vestry is low, flat-roofed and rather insignificant, but its pointed windows and sandstone walls match the rest of the building. Inside the finishes are simple – plain plasterwork, ceilings of tongue-and-groove boards, and a mixture of stone and timber floors. The building gives the impression of a simple country church with none of the decorative extravagance that is seen in 19th-century churches on the British mainland – and it is none the worse for that.

Opposite A grave in the churchyard, marked by a large stone cross.

Left The tracery patterns on the church's pulpit and lectern are actually more ornate than the simple tracery in its windows.

Above This view shows the nave looking east. At the far end, the east window is made up of a trio of tall, pointed windows known as lancets. Windows like this were typical of 13th-century church architecture and became a popular motif when the Gothic style was revived.

The parish church served Cushendun well for some 160 years, but by the dawn of the new millennium the congregation in this small community had fallen to an unsustainable level. Locals tried to keep it open, but by 2003 the congregation had joined their neighbours at Layde church in nearby Cushendall, and Cushendun's church was deconsecrated. The graveyard, though, remains consecrated ground, still in use and well cared for by the voluntary Cushendun Churchyard Care Group. Whatever the eventual fate of the church, the group will continue their work in the churchyard.

So the church has stood empty and unused for several years. From the outside it still looks in fair condition. The nave roof-covering is still sound – though its life is limited now – and the walls are generally solid. But there are plenty of problems. As Kerry Goyer, who became involved with the church through the Churchyard Care Group, explains: 'Inside there is one bad crack, the plaster is peeling and one stained-glass window

is broken. The interior looks dilapidated but it is rescuable.' In addition, the vestry roof needs recovering and damage by woodworm needs treating.

It is the usual catalogue of problems that occur in an unused building but at Cushendun they are not too far advanced. If action is taken soon a great deal of further decay will be prevented and money will be saved. One hurdle has already been overcome. When the original owners – the Whites, McNeills and MacDonnells – gave the land for the church, a clause in the deeds stated that in the event of deconsecration the land should revert to the families who gave it. But the families' present-day representatives have waived their rights to the land, leaving the way open for the formation of a Buildings Preservation Trust to take care of the church.

The needs of the structure itself – the roofing work, plastering, pointing, repairs to the windows and so on – are already largely known and plans are also underway to provide some

additional facilities, including heating, lighting and toilets, that will make the building more suitable for a variety of functions.

This is the key to the building's survival. Kerry Goyer stresses that the community is keen to preserve the integrity of the building: 'There was once a plan to turn it into apartments but we do not need more apartments in Cushendun. And we want to find a use that preserves the building's form and keeps it open to the public. An arts centre housing a range of activities from exhibitions to dance classes seems the best option.'

In centuries gone by the church was the centre of any village. It housed all sorts of functions, from local meetings and courts to schools and charitable works. The former parish church at Cushendun now has the chance to be reclaimed by the community. Several local groups have already expressed an interest in using the building for a range of functions, including evening classes, concerts, lectures and exhibitions. School projects and a film club showing classic films, world cinema and other releases not normally seen in commercial cinemas may also be added. Both yoga groups and performers of traditional music have expressed an interest, and there is the potential to use this lovely building as a wedding venue – a function that could provide valuable income with which to maintain the church.

Such a facility could provide huge value for the village. Local amenities have been slowly disappearing over the years: one of the two shops has gone and two of the three hotels. And now that Cushendun houses many people who commute to nearby towns a central gathering place will be an extra bonus – one that keeps more people in the village and sustains the community. When Clough Williams-Ellis laid out his houses in the early 20th century he also hoped to build a village hall. These plans did not bear fruit and the restoration of the church could help fill that gap at last. ■

Above Looking west along the small nave, the space is dominated by its white walls and timber-framed roof. At the far end is the door through which parishioners enter via the tower.

Former Parish Church, Cushendun

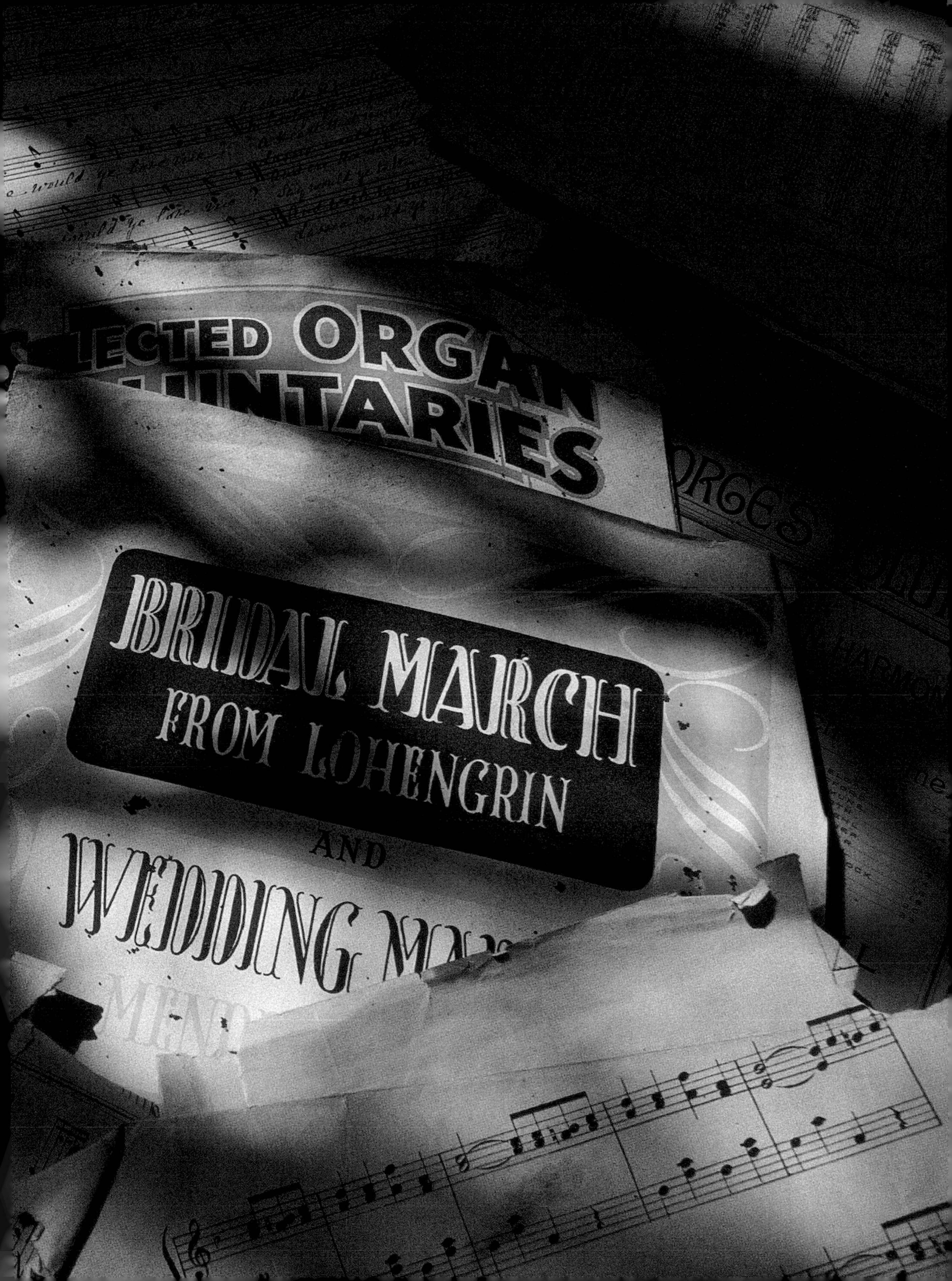
ORGAN
BRIDAL MARCH
FROM LOHENGRIN
AND
WEDDING

Old Primary School, Gracehill

Index

Figures in **bold** refer to illustrations outside of main entries

English Heritage Image References

Introduction
12l AA058845; 12m AA058758;
12r AA148297; 13l AA059726;
13r AA059135; 14l AA059659;
14r AA059653

Chapter 1
16 AA058790; 17t AA058995;
17b AA058843; 19t AA058786;
19bl AA059000; 19br AA058849;
20 AA059794; 21 AA059829;
22 AA058789; 23 AA058806;
24t AA058820; 24b AA058816;
25 AA058819; 26 AA059211;
27 AA058987; 28 AA058997;
29l AA058983; 29r AA058981;
30t AA058999; 30b AA059213;
31 AA058986; 32 AA058860;
33 DP059013; 34 AA058864;
35l DP059014; 35r AA058837;
36t AA058842; 36b AA058840;
37 AA058861; 38–9 AA058993;
40 AA058796; 41 AA058844

Chapter 2
42 DP005620; 43t AA058866;
43b AA058720; 44l AA058676;
44r AA058881; 45 AA058731;
46 AA058673; 47 AA058685;
48tl AA058688; 48tr AA058699;
48bl AA058695; 48br AA058682;
49 AA058674; 50 AA058678;
51 AA058701; 52 AA058880;
53 AA058867; 54 AA058871;
55l AA058882; 55r AA058883;
56 AA058869; 57t AA058901;
57b AA058886; 58 AA058720;
59 AA058739; 60 AA058727;
61tl AA058702; 61tr AA058706;
62 AA058735; 63t AA058737;
63bl AA058719; 63bm AA058749;
63br AA058713; 64–5 AA058692;
66 AA058747; 67 AA058902

Chapter 3
68 AA059807; 69t AA059913;

69b AA048282; 70t AA059752;
70l AA059931; 70r AA048302;
72 AA059800; 73 AA059768;
74t AA059764; 74b AA059762;
75 AA059809; 76tl AA059787;
76tr AA059797; 76bl AA059815;
76br AA059776; 77t AA059769;
77b AA059770; 78 AA059917;
80tl AA059929; 80tr AA059921;
80b AA059911; 81t AA059939;
81b AA059938; 82 AA059932;
83l AA059934; 83r AA059926;
84 AA048303; 85 AA048301;
86 AA048280; 87t AA048292;
87b AA048308; 88t AAAA048290;
88b AA048310; 89t AA048284;
89b AA048278; 90 AA059763;
91 AA059935; 92–3 AA048293

Chapter 4
94 AA059689; 95t DP005769;
95b AA059748; 96 AA059669;
97l DP005704; 97r AA059737;
98 AA059674; 99 AA059697;
100t AA059685; 100b AA059692;
101t AA059670; 101b AA059682;
102 AA059691; 103l AA059675;
103r AA059681; 104 DP005731;
105 DP005764; 106 DP005698;
107t DP005695; 107b AA059733;
108t AA059705; 108b AA059707;
109t AA059737; 109b AA059723;
110 AA059733; 111 AA059732;
112t AA059711; 112b AA059725;
113 AA059699; 114 AA059731;
115l AA059719; 115r AA059721;
116 DP005746; 117 AA059678;
118–19 AA059728

Chapter 5
120 AA059133; 121t AA059873;
121b DP005796; 123t AA059124;
123bl AA059890; 123br AA059159;
124 AA059130; 125 DP005826;
126 AA059131; 127 AA059118;
128 AA059137; 129l AA059125;

129r AA059138; 130 AA059872;
131 AA059882; 132 AA059889;
133tl AA059886; 133tr AA059887;
133bl AA059895; 133 brAA059909;
134 AA059906; 135 AA059878;
136 AA059170; 137 AA059157;
138 DP005795; 139tl AA059174;
139tr AA059161; 139bl AA059163;
139br AA059175; 140t AA059165;
140b AA059148; 141 AA059146;
142–3 AA059905; 144 AA059168;
145 AA059122

Chapter 6
146 AA059616; 147t DP005979;
147b AA059573; 148 AA059655;
149l DP005971; 149r AA059591;
150 AA059611; 152 AA059635;
153t AA059628; 153b AA059624;
154l AA059634; 154r AA059621;
155l AA059636; 155r AA059641;
156 DP005986; 157 AA059999;
158t AA059967; 158b AA059998;
159 AA059977; 160 AA059032;
161l AA059011; 161r AA059037;
162l AA059590; 162r AA059583;
163 AA059582; 164t AA059584;
164b AA059569; 165 AA059594;
166l AA059600; 166r AA059603;
167t AA059607; 167m AA059608;
167b AA059602; 168 DP005975;
169 AA059589; 170–1 AA059654

Chapter 7
172 AA059948; 173 AA059977;
174l AA059969; 174r AA059996;
175 AA059993; 176 AA059956;
178t AA059965; 178l AA059974;
178r AA059962; 179 AA059950;
180t AA059964; 180b AA059955;
181 AA059970; 182 AA059983;
183 AA059980; 184 AA059979;
185 AA059987; 186 AA059984;
187 AA059986; 188–9 AA059992;
190–1 AA059961

Useful Addresses

Ancient Monuments Society
St Ann's Vestry Hall
2 Church Entry
London
EC4V 5HB
020 7236 3934
www.ancientmonumentssociety.org.uk

Architects Accredited in Building Conservation
11 Oakfield Road
Poynton
Cheshire
SK12 1AR
01625 871458
www.aabc-register.co.uk

Architectural Heritage Fund
Alhambra House
27–31 Charing Cross Road
London
WC2H OAU
020 7925 0199
www.ahfund.org.uk

Association of Building Preservation Trusts
Clareville House
26–7 Oxendon Street
London
SW1Y 4EL
020 7930 1629
www.heritage.co.uk/apt

Building Conservation Directory
Cathedral Communications
High Street
Tisbury
Wiltshire
SP3 6HA
01747 871717
www.buildingconservation.com

Cadw
Crown Building
Cathays Park
Cardiff
CF1 3NQ
01222 500200
www.cadw.wales.gov.uk

Civic Trust
Essex Hall
1–6 Essex Street
London
WC2R 3HU
Tel 020 7539 7900
www.civictrust.org.uk

English Heritage
1 Waterhouse Square
138–42 Holborn
London
EC1 2ST
020 7973 3000
www.english-heritage.org.uk

Georgian Group
6 Fitzroy Square
London
W1T 5DX
020 7529 8920
www.georgiangroup.org.uk

Historic Scotland
Longmore House
Salisbury Place
Edinburgh
EH9 1SH
0131 668 8600
www.historic-scotland.gov.uk

Institute of Historic Building Conservation
Jubilee House
High Street
Tisbury
Wiltshire
SP3 6HA
01747 873133
www.ihbc.org.uk

National Monument Record Centre
English Heritage
Kemble Drive
Swindon
SN2 2GZ
01793 414600
www.english-heritage.org.uk

National Trust
Heelis
Kemble Drive
Swindon
SN2 2NA
01793 817400
www.nationaltrust.org.uk

National Trust for Scotland
Wemyss House
28 Charlotte Square
Edinburgh
EH2 4ET
0131 243 9300
www.nts.org.uk

Royal Institute of British Architects
66 Portland Place
London
W1B 1AD
020 7580 5533
www.riba.org

Royal Institute of Structural Engineers
11 Upper Belgrave Street
London
SW1X 8BH
020 7235 4535
www.istructe.org.uk

Royal Institution of Chartered Surveyors
RICS Contact Centre
Surveyor Court
Westwood Way
Coventry
CV4 8JE
0870 333 1600
www.rics.org

SAVE Britain's Heritage
77 Cowcross Street
London
EC1M 6EJ
020 7253 3500
www.savebritainsheritage.org

Society for the Protection of Ancient Buildings
37 Spital Square
London
E1 6DY
020 7377 1644
www.spab.org.uk

Scottish Civic Trust
The Tobacco Merchants House
42 Miller Street
Glasgow
G1 1DT
0141 221 1466
www.scotnet.co.uk/sct

Twentieth Century Society
70 Cowcross Street
London
EC1M 6EJ
020 7250 3857
www.c20society.org.uk

Ulster Architectural Heritage Society
66 Donegall Pass
Belfast
BT7 1BU
Northern Ireland
028 9055 0213
www.uahs.co.uk

Victorian Society
1 Priory Gardens
Bedford Park
London
W4 1TT
020 8994 1019
www.victorian-society.org.uk

Weald and Downland Open Air Museum
Singleton
Chichester
West Sussex
PO18 OEU
01243 811363
www.wealddown.co.uk

West Dean College
West Dean
Chichester
West Sussex
PO18 OQZ
01243 811301
www.westdean.org.uk